Soviet Afghan Relations

Dr. SATISH GANJOO

1990

Akashdeep Publishing House
DELHI

First Published 1990

ISBN 81-7158-100-5

Published by
Akashdeep Publishing House
1-7A, New Govind Pura, Near Chander Nagar,
Delhi-110 051.
Phone 3261597

Printed at :
Sangita Printers
Maujpur, Delhi-53

SOVIET AFGHAN RELATIONS

To my Wife

Kaushilya

for her fortitude and individualism

Preface

Imperialists have always ignored the best perspectives of Soviet foreign policy and peddled the theories of *Soviet Expansionism* and the *Russian bear dancing down to the warm waters.* The traditional Soviet-Afghan relations have always been the target of imperialist propaganda. The recent development in Afghanistan have been exploited by the advocates of capitalism and neo-colonialism. They forget that Great Britain had crippled the Afghan foreign policy for about 30 years (1890-1919). It was young and dynamic Amanullah Khan, ruler of Afghanistan 1919-1929, who counteracted the British imperialism and recaptured the right to conduct his own foreign relations. Soviet Russia, by its prompt action, became the first nation to recognize the independence and sovereignty of Afghanistan. In his letter to Amanullah, May 27, 1919, Lenin expressed the hope that Afghanistan will emerge as a independent nation and uphold its freedom against foreign oppression. In his historic massage to the people of the East in the 2nd All-Russian Congress, November 22, 1919, Lenin said: "We know that the popular masses of the East will rise as independent actors, as builders of new life... The period of awakening of the East in the contemporary revolution is being succeeded by a period in which all the Eastern people will participate in deciding the destiny of the whole world". This made a strong favourable impression on Amanullah and laid the groundwork for the close Soviet-Afghan relations.

Soviet Russia never wanted any territorial gain aganist the friendly relations with Afghanistan. The students of modern history very well remember the Utra Tagai incident of 1926. Utra Tagai was an island in Amu Darya belonging to Russia, as defined by Anglo-Russian Agreement of 1872 on the formation of frontier between Russia and Afghanistan. With the beginning of 20th century, the Afghans took over the Island inspite of Russian protests in 1906 and 1914. After the Russian Revolution, this Island became the center-revolutionary and anti-Soviet Basmachi movement. In December, 1925, Soviet army marched towards the Island. The Soviet purpose was not to occupy it, but to pressurise the Afghan outhorities to remove the notorious Basmachies from the vicinity of their border. But when this incident caused apprehension among the people of Afghanistan, Soviet Russia agreed to the Afghan ownership of the Island and recognized the importance of the predominating economic advantage of the Island to that country. Soviet Russia never wanted to make contemporary Afghan issue a problem resulting in hostilities between the two countries.

The development of any human society depends on the gradual transformation from an absolete and outdated socio-economic formation to a more progressive one. But the imperialist and reactionary forces in Afghanistan, who held the masses in their grip, never wanted any change in their traditional socio-economic formation, because that meant a blow to their interests. The country was confined to the feudal stage of socio-economic formation and the imperialists wanted her to retain it. Installation of a bandit, Bach-i-Saqao on the Afghan throne in 1929 was a triumph for the imperialist, conservative and reactionary forces.

However, atleast the Soviet approach and disposition to so close a neighbour as Afghanistan was carefully noted by progressive elements in that country. The qualitative change from an exploited nation to an increasingly self-reliant one could not go unnoticed.

To understand the present crisis in Afghanistan, it is significant to study the Soviet-Afghan relations since 1919-1945. The present study is an attempt in that. The treaties, agreements, and protocols signed between the two countries during the period have also been included in this work.

Many persons deserve my sincere thanks for their considerations in the preparation of this book. My greatest debt in undertaking this work is owed to my esteemed teacher, Dr. Z.L. Jala. I greatly acknowledge his interest in research, thorough understanding and grip over the subject.

I greatefully acknowledge the kind gesture shown by Dr. B.K. Deambi and Shri J.L. Bhan. I also feel beholden to Professor S. Maqbul Ahmad, Professor Manzoor Shah, Professor A.M. Mattoo and Dr. K.N. Pandita for their thoughtful appreciation. I record my profound gratitute to my colleagues and students for their suggestions and comments, which have proven rewarding in many ways.

I have been benefited adequately from the encouragement and affection received from my parents, younger brothers and little sister. The cooperation received from them has been of immense help. My wife has also made her contribution to the success of this work in a number of ways. I feel highly thankful to all of them.

My son, Sunny, has grown alongwith my move into this venture. He has confronted with the anguish due to lack of my attention, affection and love; for which I am indebted to him. He deserve my sincere thanks and heartfelt gratitude.

Dr. Satish Ganjoo

Centre of Central Asian Studies,
University of Kashmir,
Srinagar—190006 (INDIA)

Contents

1

Introduction

Contacts between the Russians and the people of Asia began as early as 10th century AD. The Russians were interested in three Asiatic areas :

(i) Central Asian Khanates extended to Afghanistan, Sinkiang and Tibet;

(ii) Transcaucasia, Asiatic Turkey and Persia;

(iii) North Asia, Siberia and Maritime Provinces.

However, from the 13th to 15th centuries, which was the period of Tatar or Mongol invasions, the Russions came into close touch with Asian politics and its customs.

Russian expansion started in 1482 AD, when Ivan III became the Czar[1] of Russia and for the first time united the small territories.[2] The Czarist Russia had three main interests in Asia :

(i) Exploitation of Asian economic potentials;

(ii) Enhancement of Russian military and political prestige;

(iii) Need for warm water ports.

Russia also had a desire for protection and security of her territory. Peter the Great had explorations and movements made into the territories between the Black Sea and the Caspian.[3] According to the British sources, he had a desire to reach the far away India through the Central Asian Khanates.[4]

Trade and diplomatic relations between the Central Asian Khanates and Russia were of a regular nature from the second half of the 16th century. In the 17th century, these relations developed stronger and the Czarist government provided full concessions to the people of Central Asia to settle in Siberia. During the 18th and 19th centuries these relations were further strengthened. It was during the second half of 19th century that Russian influence spread throughout the Central Asian region and Czar became the paramount power. The period was of great significance in the economic structure of Russia. There was rapid increase in capitalism with the result that there arose the problem of markets. The need to capture Central Asia as external market for textiles, silk and other goods was seriously felt in the Russian industrial circles. The region also occupied a very important position because the old trade routes between Far East, China and the West ran through it. In 1849, Chikhachov, a famous Russian traveller and geographer, sought the establishment of trade relations with Central Asia to take advantage of the Anglo-American absence in this region.[5] Russia began to feel seriously that its future lie in Asia and not in Europe. Great Britain was also told that it should recognize the Russian interests in Asia. Principal purpose of the Czarist policy was to strengthen the influence of Russian history, trade and culture in Central Asia.

Before the Russian conquest, Central Asia consisted of three Khanates—Bukhara, Khiva and Kokand. As a result of the first step of Russian expansion, pressure increased on the Kokand Khanate. In 1865, Tashkent was captured by unauthorized action, and in August 1866 it was declared the part of Russia.[6] Alarmed by the annexation of Tashkent, Amir of Bukhara declared a holy war against Russia in March 1868.

But he was defeated and Samarqand lost to him. A Treaty was signed between the two states by which Bukhara was reduced to vassalage and Russia got highly favourable trade terms. In 1873, Khiva was also forced to accept the terms dictated by Russia. Even the ruler of Khiva was forced to renounce all direct and friendly relations with neighbouring territories. In this way Czarist Russia dominated all the three Khanates by concluding typical colonial treaties.

On March 2, 1876, Kokand was absorbed into the Czarist Russian empire and renamed as Ferghana Province. In 1877 Turkmen was annexed and in 1884 Merv added to the Czarist Empire by skilful diplomacy. Thus the major part of Central Asia was annexed to extend Czar's colonial policy. However, the result of this annexation was that the people of Central Asia joined the oppressed people of Russia in the revolutionary movement against the Czarist regime and contributed their share to the extraordinary success in overthrowing it.

Modern Afghanistan emerged in 1747 AD when Ahmad Shah Abdali unified different autonomous tribes to give the country a definite shape. But the position of this little kingdom remained like a wreched boat in the vast stormy ocean of power rivalry, tossed here and there, and likely to be crashed against the rocks of Anglo-Czarist imperialism at any movement. Strategic considerations and trade interests were the causes of Anglo-Russian rivalry in the region. Czarist Russia subjected Afghanistan to pressure by pushing ruthlessly down the north and Great Britain by moving towards the country from the east.[7] Britain was interested in acquiring colonies and tried to increase its influence in Iran, Central Asia and China. Afghanistan, which formed the heart of Asia, was the best seat as a powerful springboard for military and political penetration of the British.[8] They also never wanted that any country should have the advantage of approaching the frontiers of their Indian colony. Both the rivals, Great Britain and Czarist Russia, were interested in the sources of raw material for their capitalist industries and the market for the commodities produced by these industries.

Great Britain was more concerned about Afghanistan and wanted to make it a base to penetrate into Turkmenia. With this purpose, Britain waged the First Afghan War in 1839-42, when Russia was not so much involved in Central Asia. In 1869, when Sher Ali became Amir of Afghanistan, Britain tried to win him over to their side but the negotiations failed.

The British authorities wanted to halt the Czarist expansion at the River Oxus because of their suspicion of growing Russian interests in Afghanistan, and the so-called security of their Indian colony. In 1869, negotiations started between Great Britain and Russia to create a neutral zone in Central Asia and to prevent the annexation of Afghanistan by any of the two rivals. Russia demanded to include Afghanistan in the proposed neutral zone. Finally in 1873, an Agreement was concluded which established the northern frontiers of Afghanistan.[9] By this Agreement, Russia declared Afghanistan outside her sphere of influence and liquidated the British opposition in the conquest of Khiva. Afghanistan was considered as an "idle buffer state" and its independence was needed by both sides.

In 1875, when the threat of Germany in the competition for world markets increased, Russia joined hands with Great Britain. But for the sphere of influence in Afghanistan, both powers remained hostile to each other. The British influence was increasing in Iran and Afghanistan. In 1878, the British were preparing to enter Afghanistan and it was planned to create a separate state of west Afghan kingdom, dependent on British support, consisting of Merv, Balkh, Kandhar and Herat.[10]

For the security of India against the so-called aggressive designs of Russia, the British Indian authorities waged Second Afghan War in 1879-81. At that time India was suffering from great famine, which took a tool of five million human lives. Millions of Indians were dying due to plague and hunger when a magnificent "Durbar" was held at Delhi for the glory of the Great British Empire. Millions of rupees were spent on the Afghan War. After the war, Treaty of Gandamuk was concluded by which Afghanistan lost her sovereignty and turned into a colonial appendage of the British Indian Empire. It was after this war that Afghanistan was forced to accept the British control on its foreign policy.

Russia annexed Turkmenia and Merv to thwart Britain from going north beyond Afghanistan. Inspired by the British, the Afghan forces marched into the Oasis of Panjdeh in 1884. The area was inhabited by Turkmens. The Afghans were defeated by the Russian forces. An Agreement was concluded between Great Britain and Czarist Russia, which was given effect by a Protocol signed in London on September 10, 1885, by virtue of which Panjdeh Oasis was recognized as a Russian possession, while Russia handed over Zulfiqar region to Afghanistan.[11] The boundary of this region was demarcated during 1886-88 by an Anglo-Russian Commission, not by Russo-Afghan Commission, which reveal that the Afghans were completely treated as serviles.

In 1883, Afghan troops were sent to occupy Shugnan and Rushan. The Russian government protseted against the Afghan action. But the British authorities replied that the Afghans consider Shugnan and Rushan as the parts of Badakshan given to it by the Agreement of 1873. Russia, being engaged in Turkmenia, could not pursue the matter further. In 1888, internal troubles broke out in Afghanistan and the people of Shugnan sought the help of Russia to establish their own rule. However, the uprising was suppressed by Amir Abdur Rahman.

In 1895, Shugnan and Rushan were ceded to Russia. A part of Darwaz, on the left bank of the Amu Darya, was given to Afghanistan. A joint Anglo-Russian Commission created an eight mile wide arm of Afghanistan reaching out to touch China as the buffer between British India and Russia. In 1896, the frontier between Russia and Afghanistan was settled.

Minor adjustments of frontier between the two countries took place in 1920s, 1930s and 1946.

In 1907 Anglo-Russian rivalry over Afghan issue was settled when Russia declared Afghanistan outside its sphere of influence and agreed to conduct all political relations through the British agencies.[12] Commercial facilities were equally open to both the powers. The Afghans never recognized the Anglo-Russian Convention of 1907 concerning Afghanistan. But they were forced to be silent.

Czar not only caused the fear in the neighbouring countries, but also oppressed the people of his own country—Russia. Capitalism, feudalism and imperialism developed to a considerable extent in Russia. There were capitalist exploitations in the Khanates of Central Asia also. All this resulted in industrial crisis, and also of peasant and workers unrest. In this state of confusion, Lenin[13] came forward as a great revolutionary and originated the revolutionary working-class movement. In the very beginning of 20th century, Czar saw the open and ruthless class struggle. In 1904, Russia was full of crises and struggles. The defeat of Russia by Japan adversely affected Czarist influence, both inside and outside the country.[14] The revolutionary movement spread far beyond the small groups of the underground socialist parties.[15] Lenin believed that the military defeat of autocracy has produced the effect of Russian freedom.

The first Russian Revolution began in 1905-07. It proved an outstanding event in the history of Russia. Lenin described it as the "dress rehearsal" for the Revolution of 1917. The years from 1907 to 1914 saw the clear sings of new historical trends in the socio-political life of Russia. The working class movement gained strong grounds. In 1914, First World War broke out and Russia joined the Entente. Russian people opposed the Czar for joining the war. Economic and political chaos deepened in the country. Capitalism and exploitation continued to grow decisively and at a terrific speed. Lenin's activities became intensive and he gave the cry for socialism.

In 1915, strikes and demonstrations started which acquired political dimension. The revolutionary activities against Czar also began in Uzbekistan, Kirghizia, Turkmenia and Kazakhistan. The year 1917 ushered in an unprecedented wave of strikes and ultimately, on 3rd March, Czar abdicated and power passed into the hands of the revolutionaries.

With the formation of Soviet Union, a fundamentally new foreign policy was inaugurated which recognized the full equality of the people of the East and provided for friendly support to these people against imperialist expansion. On Lenin's initiative, Soviet Russia declared a complete break with the barbarous policy of bourgeois civilization, which had built the prosperity of the exploiters belonging to a few chosen nations on the enslavement of hundreds of millions of working people in small countries.[16]

In a short period of history, the oppressed people of Central Asia succeeded in completing the transition from pre-capitalist society to advanced socialism, by-passing the long and painful stage of capitalism. The Soviet policy towards nationalities in Central Asia was the encouragement and promotion of national and linguistic distinctions of the people within the overall socialist set up.[17] The ideology of Lenin strongly supported internal freedom of the Central Asian nationalities and even some of them were granted autonomous status.[18]

Afghanistan is politically, socially, culturally and commercially linked with Central Asia. There are the Tadjiks and Uzbeks in Northern Afghanistan, who are linked by blood relationships with the people of Tadjikistan and Uzbekistan. So the political developments in Central Asia influenced the political scenario in Afghanistan. Desire of the nationalist Afghans to secure complete sovereignty and independence was accelerated by the Russia Revolution of 1917. The Afghans became concious that unless they combined socio-economic development with political independence, the future of their country was in peril.[19] In February, 1919, Amir Habibullah wrote a letter to the Viceroy of India, in which he demanded the recognition of the absolute liberty, freedom of action and perpetual independence of Afghanistan.[20]

Amanullah Khan, who ascended the throne in 1919, courageously declared the independence and sovereignty of Afghanistan. On March 27, 1919, Soviet Russia recognized the sovereignty of Afghanistan and diplomatic relations were established between the two countries.

References

1. *Czar*, the title used by the Emperors of Imperial Russia, comes from *Caesar*, the title used by the Emperors of Rome. The Russian Empress was called the *Czarina* and the crown-prince was called the *Czarevitch*.
2. J.V. Davidson—Houston, "Russia in Asia", *Journal of Royal Central Asian Society*, Vol. 33, 1946, p. 358.
3. X. J. Eudin and R.C. North, *Soviet Russia and the East*, California, 1964, p. 5.
4. *Khanates* were the Principalities of Central Asia, ruled by *Khans* in the 19th century.
5. Devendra Kaushik, *Central Asia in the Modern Times*, Moscow, 1970, pp. 29-33.
6. *Ibid.*, pp. 44-46.
7. Donald N. Wilber, "Afghanistan : Independent and Encircled", *Foreign Affairs*, April, 1953, p. 486.
8. P.N. Fedoseyev (ed.), *Afghanistan: Past and Present*, Moscow, 1981, p. 99.
9. Devendra Kaushik, *op. cit.*, p. 51.
10. Lady Betty Balfour, *The History of Lord Lytton's Indian Administration*, London, 1899, p. 247.
11. Devendra Kaushik, *op. cit.*, pp. 57-58.
12. Donald N. Wilber, *op. cit.*, p. 487.
13. Born on April 10 (22), 1870, in the town of Simbirsk (now Ulyanovsk), Vladimir Ilyich Ulyanov-Lenin, made a profound study of the writings of Marx and Engels, and took the revolutionary road of struggle. He tried to make the people politically conscious and for this purpose founded the newspaper *Iskara* in 1900. His book *What is to be done*? (1902) formulated the new ideological and organisational principles of working class, I.I. Smirnow, *A Short History of the U.S.S.R.*, Part I, Moscow, 1965, pp. 290-292. For details see Louis Fischer, *The Life of Lenin*, New York, 1964.

14. V.I. Lenin, *Collected Works*, Russian Edition, IV, p. 165.
15. David J. Dallin, *The Rise of Russia in Asia*, London, 1950, p. 79.
16. V.I. Lenin, *Collected Works*, Vol. XXVI, p. 424.
17. For an outline of the Soviet nationalities policy, See R. Vaidynath, *The Formation of the Soviet Central Asian Republics*, New Delhi, 1929, pp. 250-265.
18. After the formation of Soviet Russia, the Central Asia was re-organized into the five Republics :
    1. The Uzbek S.S.R. (Uzbekistan), formed on October 27, 1924, capital : Tashkent, Area, 447.4 thousand square kms.
    2. The Kazakh S.S.R. (Kazakhistan), formed on December 5, 1936, Capital : Alma Ata, Area 2,717.3 thousand square kms.
    3. The Kirghiz S.S.R. (Kirghizia), formed on December 5, 1936, Capital : Frunze, Area : 198.5 thousand square kms.
    4. The Tadjik S.S.R. (Tadjikistan), formed on October 16, 1929 : Capital : Dushambe, Area : 143.1 thousand square kms.
    5. The Turkmen S.S.R. (Turkmenia), formed on October 27, 1924, Capital : Ashkhabad, Area : 488.1 thousand square kms.
19. Clive J. Roome, "The Future of Afghanistan", *The Near East*, March 7, 1919, p. 209.
20. Amalendu Guha (ed.), *Central Asia*, Delhi, 1970, p. 265.

2

Quest for Coexistence

The German efforts to drag Afghanistan into the World War failed despite a secret Treaty between the two countries concluded on January 24, 1916.[1] It was the Great Socialist Revolution in Russia which caused the fundamental changes in the Afghan nationalism and created the favourable conditions for throwing off the British imperialism.

On February 20, 1919, Habibullah was assassinated and his brother, Nasrullah, proclaimed himself Amir of Afghanistan.[2] But Amanullah Khan—the young, dynamic, ambitious and popular son of the late Amir—who was a symbol of nationalism and progress, ascended the throne on February 25, 1919.[3] Only after three days, on February 28, Amanullah proclaimed the sovereignty of Afghanistan. As an initial move, the messages were sent to the governments of Japan, Soviet Russia, United States, France, Iran, Turkey and other countries announcing the accession of Amanullah and his desire to establish friendly relations with these countries.[4]

With the emergence of Amanullah, a new chapter was started in the Soviet-Afghan relations. No doubt, in 1901-1903, Czarist Russia had tried to establish diplomatic relations with Afghanistan, but British domination on Afghan foreign policy had been a big hurdle in the way.[5] However, on 7th April, 1919, Amanullah sent a message to Moscow, expressing the desire to establish friendly relations.[6] Soviet Russia was the first country to be approached by Afghanistan. No doubt the general feeling among the Afghans at this time was that Soviet Russia wanted to add Afghanistan to its Turkestan province.[7] Inspired by the British, the conservative and the fundamentalist forces in Afghanistan propagated that Soviet Russia was the greatest and most dangerous enemy of Islam.

The Afghan message was delivered to Moscow on May 21, 1919, and Soviet Russia accelerated to make its relations cordial with Afghanistan.[8] In their reply of May 27, 1919, Lenin and Kalinin congragulated Amanullah and formally recognized the independence of Afghanistan. After Afghanistan, Estonia was the second country with which Soviet Russia established friendly relations.

The Soviet message to Afghanistan stated : "In reply to the first message to be issued by Afghanistan as a free and independent nation, conveying greetings to the Russian people and announcing Your Majesty's accession to the throne, we hasten to convey the greetings of the workers' and peasants' Government and the entire people of Russia to the independent Afghan people, who are heroically upholding their freedom against foreign oppression.... We welcome Your Majesty's intention to built close relations with the Russian people, and request you to appoint an official representative in Moscow. For our part, we are prepared to despatch a representative of the Workers' and Peasants' Government to Kabul, and request that Your Majesty order the authorities concerned to facilitate his journey. Establishment of permanent diplomatic relations between the two great nations will present broad opportunities for mutual assistance against any encroachment by foreign forces on their freedom."[9]

Indian revolutionaries played a very important part in the establishment of Soviet-Afghan relations and made a substantial contribution in the establishment of direct contacts between the Eastern People and Soviet Russia. Mahendra Pratap, who came to Afghanistan with German representatives during First World War, Barkatullah and Obaidullah Sindhi had formed the Provincial Independent Government of India in Kabul on 1st December, 1915, acting as President, Prime Minister and Foreign Minister.[10] They were extended patronage and monetary benefit by Nasrullah—then the leader of the anti-British group at the Afghan court. Barkatullah was also received by Lenin in Moscow on May 7, 1919, as Afghanistan's first unofficial representative.[11] Earlier, in March 1919, Barkatullah had written a Persian pamphlet, *Bolshevism and the Islamic Nations*, in which he explained the Marxist-Socialism as a return of the concept of the *bayat-al-mal*, the common treasury for the whole community, and it was explained to the Muslims that they should join with Soviet Russia against the British imperialism.[12] In July, 1919, Lenin received more Indians—Mahendra Pratap, Abdur Rab Barg, P. Acharya, Dalip Singh Gill and others.[13]

The Third Anglo-Afghan war started on May 3, 1919. Soviet Russia offered friendly help and assistance to Afganistan. Great Britain, which had emerged victorious in First World War, met with reverses in Afghanistan. However, both sides agreed to cease hostalities. Britain recognized the independence and sovereignty of Afghanistan in domestic and foreign affairs, the fundamental cause of the British defeat was that its army was still engaged in the developments of World War.[14] There also took place an insurgency in the Punjab which handicapped the British authorities.

After getting success in the "War of Independence" (1919), Amanullah began to sympathise with the Indian people. Leaflets were distributed in north-west India which inspired the Indians to revolt against Rowlatt Act.[15] When the Indian Khilafatists made common cause with the Indian National Congress, who at that time had launched non-cooperation movement; Amanullah promised them for help and support. Some 18,000 Khilafatists left British India for Afghanistan, when a call was given to them to leave the country and join Kamal Pasha's army in Turkey (Hijrat Movement). By 1920, it swept away more than 36,000 people from India to Afghanistan. On April 18, 1920, a Khilafat Conference was held in Delhi, in which the *farman* of Amanullah was also read out. Though the circumstances compelled Indian emigrants to return home, even then a group of these emigrants settled in different parts of Central Asia.

A 19-member delegation was appointed by Amanullah to represent Afghanistan in Paris Peace Conference.[16] The Afghan mission included Muhammad Wali Khan, Kazim Bey, Faiz Muhammad Khan, Ebib Effedi, a number of secretaries and translators. Ghulam Siddiq Khan joined it later. The Afghan delegation crossed the Soviet-Afghan border in May 28, 1919, and arrived in Tashkent on June 4. The delegation was cordially received at Tashkent and was allowed to establish an Afghan Consulate there headed by Muhammad Aslam Khan.[17] In the opening speech, Muhammad Aslam Khan said that to find the salvation of Muslims all over the world, Afghans have made friendship with Soviet Russia. He also advised the people of Soviet Central Asia to prefer Soviet copper to British gold.

Afghans wanted to conclude an alliance with the Soviets to avoid British imperialism and outbreak of another Anglo-Afghan war. In this connection, a Soviet representative, Y.Z. Suritz, had already made a visit to Afghanistan during the summer of 1919.[18] In August, Leon Trotsky made enquiries regarding the military conditions and material needs in Afghanistan, and also reliability of Amanullah. A message from Moscow indicated that Afghanistan would receive free military aid after the railroad links with Tashkent were established.[19] The aeroplanes were to be despatched in near future.

Leaving Tashkent on 24th September, 1919, the Afghan mission arrived in Moscow on October 10. Owing to political disturbances raging on all sides, it took 13 days for the Afghan mission to reach Moscow from Tashkent. Only three countries, who alone had at that time recognized Soviet regime, had their diplomatic representatives in Moscow.[20] A warm welcome was given to the Afghan mission there. N.N. Narimanov the commissariat for Foreign Affairs, said on this occasion that the Russian imperial striving to enslave and degrade small nationalities has gone for ever.[21] Sultan Galiev, Incharge of Oriental Affairs honoured the mission and said that Soviet Russia would provide all possible help and assistance to Afghanistan. In reply Muhammad Wali Khan said, "we know that the Musulman peoples of Russia are now free and we strongly hope that, with the help of Soviet Russia, we shall succeed in emancipating our Afghanistan and the rest of the East".[22] Lenin received the mission with great pleasure.

Inspired by the Britisn, Estonian government prevented the passage for Afghan mission to travel to Europe. The mission turned back from Moscow on November 27, 1919, and arrived in Tashkent on December 19.

A Soviet mission under N.Z. Bravin set out for Afghanistan and arrived in Herat in July 1919.[23] Bravin, a former Czarist Consular in Birjand (Iran), arrived in Herat alongwith 30 cavalrymen including one German and ten Austrians, who were experts in the manufacture of field equipments. It was also reported that he had got 120 poney loads of ammunition with him. The sole purpose of the mission was to initiate discussions with Afghanistan until the arrival of plenary powered Moscow mission. Bravin started negotiations with Amanullah about the Panjdeh territory.[24]

According to Soviet sources, the mission of N.Z. Bravin was attacked by the British agents, in violation of Afghanistan's sovereignty and resulted in two deaths and 18 injuries.[25] But the British are silent about the same. However, Bravin officially informed Afghan Government that Soviet Russia was prepared to make territorial concessions.

Y.Z. Suritz, the Soviet plenipotentiary Minister to

Afghanistan, left Moscow in October 1919, and reached Herat on November 11, 1919.[26] He headed the mission consisting of some twenty members—including one German, three Austrians fourteen Cossacks and three Indians. Among the Indians were Mahendra Pratap and Barakatullah, who at that time were in Moscow. They were assigned the task to introduce Suritz to Amanullah. In Afghanistan the Soviet mission was accorded an extraordinary welcome and a salute of sixty guns. In January, 1920, when the mission reached Kabul, friendly negotiations started between two countries for coexistence, non-aggression and mutual assistance. The Soviets were examining the possibilities to present Afghanistan several fleets, airplanes and much heavy artillery.[27] The purpose was to make Afghanistan proportionately resourceful to fight the British imperialism. Gradually, the Soviets came to be regarded as the friends of the Muslims.

When Suritz reached Kabul, Bravin was asked to step down. He took it as his insult and subsequently defected, becoming an Afghan citizen. But when he was about to travel to India, some unknown murderer assassinated him in Ghazni for some personal enmity.

The German member of the Suritz mission left Afghanistan after three months and carried a message to the German Foreign Minister, requesting for the posting of an official representative to Kabul and promotion of trade between the two countries.[28] Germany was destined to play a very important role in Afghanistan.

The Afghans were disturbed over the developments in their north. The Revolution in Bukhara in 1920, which brought the Amir and hundreds of his Uzbek supporters as refugees to Afghanistan, caused a revulsion of feeling against Soviet Russia among the fundamentalist and conservative forces in that country.[29] In fact, these fundamentalist and conservative forces in Afghanistan and Soviet Central Asia were inspired by the British imperialism. Soviet Russia and Great Britain were distrustful of each other also and did not maintain even diplomatic relations in 1920. However, Suritz was strictly instructed to avoid any promise to Afghanistan which would force Soviet Russia into a hostility with Britain. In fact, the Soviets hoped for western recognition and resumption of commercial relations with Great Britain.[30] In spite of its delicate relations with Great Britain, Soviet Russia wanted the deliverance of Afghanistan from imperialism and colonialism. This was the best perspective of Soviet foreign policy.

The main features of conversation between Suritz and the Afghan authorities were Soviet assistance and territorial concessions. A commercial treaty between the two countries, which was under discussion, contained the following terms and conditions:

1. Raw material and manufactured goods were to be supplied by each country;
2. The Soviets were to conduct all trade with Afghan individual merchants and the Afghan government through the Soviet Department for Foreign Trade;
3. Soviet Russia was not to impose any duty on the imports from Afghanistan.

The commercial treaty was treated by the Soviets as a preliminary to any political agreement. Amanullah asked for a treaty of friendship and mutual assistance, which was to include the following provisions :

1. The districts of Kerki and Terek to be ceded to Afghanistan;
2. Afghan representative was to be appointed in the Russo-Bukhara Commission;
3. Ten million gold roubles were to be paid as subsidy to Afghanistan;
4. An installation for the production of smokeless gun powder was to be supplied to Afghanistan;

5. Besides, Soviet Russia was to provide :

   (i) telegraph lines from Kushk to Herat directly and via Kandahar to Kabul;

   (ii) 10,000 rifles;

   (iii) civil and military interpreters;

   (iv) a number of batteries of artillery;

   (v) wireless telegraphy installations at Kabul, Herat and Kandahar;

   (vi) assistance in arming the Indian Frontier Tribes; and

   (vii) Permission to use two steamers in the River Oxus.

Suritz proposed the following provisions in this treaty of friendship and mutual assistance :

1. No agreement shall be concluded by either party which might prove injurious to the other;
2. Soviet Russia was to be kept informed of any negotiations with Britain by the Afghan authorities, which might affect Soviet Russia;
3. Soviet representative was to be recognized formally;
4. Soviet Russia was to establish factories at Kandahar, Ghazni and Jalalabad;
5. A commercial treaty was to be concluded between the two countries.

Meanwhile, the Afghan mission under the chairmanship of Muhammad Wali Khan visited different European countries, signing various treaties and agreements. In England, the members of the mission were told to negotiate directly with the British Indian authorities.[32] Afghans felt humiliated by the posture of the British. A British plot to assassinate Amanullah in June, 1920, made the Amir more anti-British than anti-Bolshevik.[33] Anglo-Afghan hostality strengthened the Afghan desire for a rapproachement with Soviet Russia.

On September 13, 1920, the two countries, Afghanistan and Soviet Russia, signed a Treaty in Kabul, which was ratified by Soviet Russia on February 28, 1921, and Afghanistan in August 1921. If not the intention, but the result of this Treaty was to resist the British imperialism.[34] For a time it seemed as if the 19th century rivalry between Russia and Great Britain was about to be resumed. It was the first equal Treaty signed by Afghanistan with any other country. This treaty brought the two countries into the sphere of active foreign policy and diplomatic relations. The provisions of the Treaty put Soviet Russia under specific obligations. By the end of 1923, the Soviets met all their aid obligations and cultivated the dynamic friendly relations with the Afghans.

Specific instructions were enunciated to the Soviet Ambassador in Afghanistan on June 3, 1921.[35] In these instructions, the Soviet Commissariat for Foreign Affairs wrote that the Soviet government was eager to facilitate the development and prosperity of Afghanistan. Despite their different social systems, Soviet Russia and Afghanistan were linked by their common aspirations for complete sovereignty and independence. Soviet Russia never wanted to interfere in the internal affairs of Afghanistan, but wanted to contribute in her process of development and self-reliance.

The victory of India was so puzzled with the conclusion of Soviet-Afghan Treaty that he urged to London to settle the question of Afghanistan with Moscow. He also put forward the proposal that Great Britain and Soviet Russia should share equal influence in Afghanistan to prevent it from playing off one European power against another. But nothing came out of these proposals. If the British authorities might had given a serious thought to the suggestions from one of their responsible officer, the situation might have been altogether different.

British imperialism played its part in strengthening the alliance and friendly relations between Soviet Russia and the oppressed people of the East.[36] Soviet Russia steadfastly supported the progressive policies of the countries that have shaken off colonialist rule. Afghan authorities were happy with the harmonious Soviet-Afghan relations. In an interview with Alice Bird, Muhammad Wali Khan said : "We are satisfied with the Russian policy. We are convinced that the policy of Russia means non-interference in the internal affairs of oriental countries. It has meant the freedom of Afghanistan."[37]

Amanullah, who was regarded as the "Soviet Trojan Horse" by the British, was seeking a balance of power in the region. He not only disarmed the Indian Revolutionaries entering Afghanistan, but also made it clear that he had no intentions of allowing the Soviet forces enter to his territory and use it as a base for so-called operation against India, as was alleged by the British. This contradicted the unconfirmed British reports that Amanullah was eager to resume hostilities with British India after the delivery of 80,000 to 1,00,000 rifles with 600 rounds per rifle; 1,500 machine guns and 50 million roubles of gold from Soviet Russia.

The Afghan mission abroad was trying to establish diplomatic relations with other countries. In the United States, where the mission reached in July 1921, negotiations were opened for establishment of diplomatic relations between the two countries.[38] The Afghans were interested in the US investment in their country. But because of close Anglo-American relations, the United States manifested very little interest in Afghanistan except trade and commerce.

Basmachi was the name given by the Soviets to an armed counter-revolutionary movement in Central Asia, which broke out in 1917 after the creation of Kokand Autonomous Republic and lasted until 1930 or even later. This movement was a rebellion by the fundamentalist and conservative people of Turkistan including feudal lords and *mullahs* against the Soviet government. It was supported and directed by Great Britain, Afghanistan and reactionary circles of other countries. The ideology of the Basmachi was pan-Islamism, pan-Turkism and bourgeoisie nationalism. They tried to convert northern Afghanistan into a springboard to penetrate into Soviet territory and create disturbances there. The Basmachi movement, establishment of Soviet rule in Bukhara in September, 1920, and flight of the Amir of Bukhara to Afghanistan offered Amanullah an opportunity to enhance his position as pan-Islamic leader. Vindicating as head of the Islamic faith, he tried to declare Afghanistan as the seat of *Khilafat* after the Turkey had collapsed as the centre of the Muslim world. Himself, Amanullah was desirous of assuming the title of *Khalifa.* He resisted the diplomatic pressure of Soviet Russia, gave refuge to the Amir of Bukhara and provided material, moral and financial assistance to the Basmachies. Soviet Russia also got interested in the pan-Islamic movement to fight the British imperialism.[39] But the activities of the Basmachi bands were unbearable for the Soviets. They got perturbed when groups and individual volunteers from Afghanistan and British India crossed Soviet-Afghan border to fiight on the side of Basmachies against Soviet Russia. Even the Afghan forces were sent to northern frontiers to await the developments.[40] Amanullah reportedly entered into secret correspondence with Envar Pasha of Turkey in 1922. However, with the death of Enver Pasha in August I922, Soviet-Afghan rivalries in Central Asia liquidated.[41]

An independent Bukhara could have served as a buffer between Soviet Russia and Afghanistan. It also could have become the centre of an Afghan-dominated Central Asian confederation. With this purpose in mind, Amanullah sent men and material to help the Bukhara in its struggle against the revolutionary forces in October 1919. Amanullah also established contacts with the British-inspired Basmachi leaders.[42] Even diplomatic relations were established between the Amir of Bukhara and Afghanistan. For the consolidation of Soviet rule in Central Asia, the Afghan-Bukharan and the

Afghan-Basmachi cooperation presented political and military menace to Soviet Russia. The Soviets were in constant threat of an Anglo-Afghan rapprochement and the possibility that Great Britain might lend political and moral support to a confederacy of anti-Soviet forces. On September 20, 1919, Trotsky wrote to the Central Committee of the Communist Party that truce between Afghanistan and Britain may wholly rebound against Soviet Russia.[43] In his opinion, Great Britain was actively engaged in uniting Iran, Bukhara, Khiva and Afghanistan against Soviet Russia. The disclosure of Amanullah's correspondence with Amir of Bukhara and his extensive contacts with the Basmachies heightened the Soviet apprehensions.[44] However, to enchant the Soviets, Amanullah disarmed about 10,000 Basmachi bandits who had fled to Afghanistan. In fact, thc main force of Basmachies melted away to form guerrila bands after the death of Enver Pasha.

Amanullah's nationalist, anti-British and pan-Islamic activities and exhortations made him famous throughout the Muslim world. Shaikh Mohammad Iqbal, the well-known philosopher poet of undivided India, dedicated his famous poem *Payam-i-Mashriq*, the message of the East, to Amanullah. These political and psychological rewards encouraged him to wash away the British imperialism in his country and develop more close relations with Soviet Russia.

According to the British secret reports, Amanullah, was not satisfied with the Soviet policy in Bukhara and other Central Asian Khanates. He was ready to break relations with Soviet Russia if Britain would agree to concede political, military and economic demands of the Afghans.[45] These demands included the British assistance of 40 lakhs of rupees; 20,000 rifles; 200 machine guns; two 18-pound batteries; ammunition; six aeroplanes; and material for a telegraph line between Kabul, Kandahar and Herat. Besides the Afghans wanted a say in the affairs of the tribal belt and assistance in the event of unprovoked Soviet aggression. But the accuracy of these reports was not established.

After the Soviet rule was established in Bukhara, Amanullah got concerned about the possibility of so-called communist revolutionary movement in Afghanistan. The British had also established the opinion that the Soviets were merely waiting for a propitious moment to liquidate Amanullah and set up a Soviet government in Kabul. The Soviets were also perplexed when they discovered some secret documents confirming the Afghan intervention in Bukhara.[46] In response to the Soviet protest, Afghanistan removed its minister in Bukhara who was at the core of mischief and recognized the Treaty between Soviet Russia and Bukhara People's Republic. With this ended the Central Asian strife between Soviet Russia and Afghanistan.

In a note dated October 9, 1920, the British Foreign Secretary, Lord Curzon, accused Soviet Russia of trying to foment an uprising of the native tribes on the Indian frontiers by signing a Treaty with the Amir of Afghanistan. British diplomatic protests and pressures compelled Amanullah to sign the Anglo-Afghan Treaty on November 22, 1921.[47] When this treaty was being negotiated by Sir H. Dobbs, he was impressed with British need for exercising arms control over Afghanistan. But he soon realised that this was impossible to secure. However, the Treaty provided the establishment of legations in London and Kabul. Afghanistan was granted tax exemptions on materials destined to help modernize the country. One of the important features of the Treaty was to keep the Soviet Consulates out of eastern Afghanistan.

Indian revolutionaries had played very important part in establishing the friendly Soviet-Afghan relations in 1919. These relations facilitated the work of these revolutionaries, functioning in Kabul, to keep contacts with the Soviet authorities and the comintern. That is why the British asked Afghanistan to expel these Indians from Kabul. With the conclusion of the Anglo-Afghan Treaty, Indian revolutionaries found it difficult to stay in Afghanistan and were ultimately expelled from that country towards the end of 1922.[48] It was on June, 17, 1922, that *Ittihad-i-Mashriqi*, the Afghan periodical, had set the tone of new Afghan foreign policy based on friendly relations with all countries. However, Amanullah continued his moral support to various pan-Islamic activities.

Before the third Anglo-Afghan war, Afghanistan met its need for weapons from Britain. But the war and other political events shattered the situation. With the result Amanullah turned towards Soviet Russia. Great Britain, realising her lost position in Afghanistan, tried hard to discourage and disturb the Soviet-Afghan relations. The British authorities wanted Afghanistan to have only trade relations with Soviet Russia. Britain even prevented the transit of arm to Afghanistan during the Anglo-Afghan crisis of 1923. But the imperialist agents soon realised that one of the functions of Afghan representative abroad was to purchase weapons and send them home by way of Soviet Russia. The Soviet arms arrived first, to be followed by consignment of Italian and French arms. But the quality of weapons was so poor that the Afghan government hesitated to accept the consignment.

Amanullah's efforts at creating an Afghan Air Force were not immediately successful. Though the Soviet and Iatlian planes arrived in Kabul, but breakage and loss of parts occurred when disassembled planes were being transported to Afghanistan. Another problem was lack of facilities and skilled personnel to man the planes. By 1923, the Afghan Air Force consisted of two Soviet and two Italian planes. At this time, an interesting incident took place. A British pilot ran over the Afghan territory and was forced to land in the area of Katawaz. The Afghan Foreign Minister graciously forgave the violation of Afghanistan's air space, telling Sir Francis Humphrys, "you keep your officer, we keep the machine." The British plane was then added to the Afghan Air Force.

Khost Rebellion broke out in Afghanistan in 1924 which

caused the downfall of Amanullah only after four years.[49] The Soviets attributed this uprising to the British imperial agents. According to the British reports, Amanullah told Sir Francis Humphrys in Kabul in an interview that his relations with Soviet Russia would have become strained, but because of Khost Rebellion, which was entirely due to the *mullah*, he was compelled to continue these ties.[50] It seems that these reports were hatched by the British authorities themselves. There was no cause for Amanullah to break the relations with Soviet Russia. However, he asked the British Indian authorities for immediate delivery of six military planes to suppress the rebellion. But to employ the British pilots was not possible. Great Britain did not allow its planes to be operated by the Soviets. However, in violation of the Article 179 of the Treaty of Versailes, the British government permitted the Germans to fly its planes in Afghanistan. In October 1924, Soviet Russia supplied five aeroplanes to Afghanistan and six more were supplied in subsequent years with pilots.[51] In fact, Afghanistan could have received Soviet planes before. But the Afghan authorities insisted that these planes be brought by road, ignoring the damage and difficulties that would occur in the process of their reassembling. By 1925, the Afghan Air Force included 26 Soviet Officers and 6 more were expected shortly. In April 1925, 20 Afghans were sent to Moscow for training in aviation.[52] Great Britain expressed its concern for employing the Soviets in the Afghanistan Air Force and considered it a threat to India. However, Amanullah assured the British that the Soviet pilots would be replaced after some other alternative arrangements.

To counter the British imperialism, Soviet presence in Afghanistan was vigorously needed.[53] Only crises in Soviet-Afghan relations were the Afghan affinities with Basmachi bands. However, on July 9, 1923, Afghan Foreign Minister, Mohammad Wali Khan, ensured Soviet Russia that the activities of Basmachi bands would be curtailed.[54] The relations between two countries continued to flourish. But these close ties were disturbed when a black-framed message was carried by a special issue of *Aman-i-Afghan* on December 19, 1925, about the invasion of Soviet troops on Afghanistan, resulting in a number of casualities. The dispute developed on "Utra Tagai" an Island circumscribed by the branches of the Amu Darya, the deeper of which was in the south and formed the boundary of Afghanistan as defined by the Agreement of 1872 between Russia and Britain. The middle of the deep stream, Thalwag, was accepted as the boundary. But at the turn of the century, it changed its course and the northern part became the main river. The Afghan moved into the area thus gained.[55] Although Russia raised the issue in 1906 and 1914, but did not propel the claim. After the Russian Revolution, about 1000 Uzbek refugees took shelter on this island, which already had a population of 150 Tadjiks. The island had also become the source of Basmachi insurrection.

The occupation of "Utra Tagai" by the Soviet troops caused great excitement in Kabul. Even Amanullah premonitioned on December 25, 1925, that hostilities might break out any time and the Afghans should be prepared to fight. The Soviet advisers to the Afghan Air Force were suspended. The Soviet survey parties working in different parts of Afghanistan were recalled to Kabul. The relations between two countries vigorously vibrated. In fact, Soviets never wanted a territorial gain against the traditional friendly relations with Afghanistan. The interests of Soviet Russia seemed to lay in the fact that it wanted to pressurise the Afghan authorities to remove notorious Basmachies from the vicinity of their border. However, because of Afghanistan's predominant economic advantages, Soviet Russia agreed to the Afghan ownership of the "Utra Tagai" Island. By February 4, 1926, the issue was debaffled by negotiations and the Soviet troops evacuated the Island on February 28.[56] On August 15, 1926, a Protocol was signed between the two countries regarding the dispute over the Island. This was followed by the Soviet-Afghan Treaty of Naturality and non-aggression concluded on August 31, 1926.

The Soviets were active in road construction and in

various engineering projects in Afghanistan. In Kabul, a radio station was built and commissioned on September 18, 1920.[57] The solitary wireless station was installed on the grounds of Dilkusha Palace in Kabul, which was operated by the Soviet and the Afghan officials. The French endeavour to instal its wireless station in Kabul was knocked back by the Afghan authorities.[58]

Amanullah, who by now had assumed the title of King, left Kabul on November 29, 1927, with the intention of visiting different countries to cultivate crony relations witn them. Leaving the kingdom in the charge of Muhammad Wali Khan, as Regent and Foreign Minister, the King left Afghanistan with his Queen and 27 members. In addition to King Amanullah and Queen Surya, the Royal Party consisted of the following :[59]

1. Prince Rahmatullah, eldest son of King and Queen.
2. Princess Nur-al-Siraj, sister of King.
3. Princess Hurya Tarzi Begum, sister of Queen.
4. Najiba Begum, half-sister of King.
5. Najia Khanum, Turkish governess.
6. Sardar Muhammad Hasan Khan, Chamberlian, husband of princess Nur-al-Siraj and first cousin of King.
7. Mahmud Beg Tarzi, Foreign Minister, father of the Queen.
8. Ghulam Siddiq Khan, Principal Private Secretary of King.
9. Muhammad Yaqub Khan, Minister of Court.
10. Sardar Sher Ahmad Khan, President of Council of State.
11. Sardar Ali Ahmad Khan, Governor of Kabul.
12. Ali Muhammad Khan, Minister in Rome.
13. Lt. Gen. Habibullah Khan, Under Secretary of War.
14. Lt. Gen. Abdur Rahman Khan, Commander, Herat Division.

15. Lt. Gen. Muhammad Umar Khan, Commander, Ist Division, Kabul Corps.

16. Brig Gen. Ghulam Dastgir Khan, Commander, Household Troops.

17. Dr. Rufqi Bey, Physician of the King.

18. Col. Abdul Tawab Khan Tarzi, Commander of Cavalry College of Kabul, brother of the Queen.

19. Ghulam Yahya Khan, Asstt. Secretary of Foreign Affairs, nephew of the Foreign Minister.

20. Muhammad Amin Khan, Asstt, Secretary of Foreign Affairs, formerly Secretary of Afghan Legation in Berlin.

21. Abdul Wahab Khan Tarzi, brother of the Queen.

22. Islam Beg Khan, Interpreter of the Afghan Legation in Paris.

23. Shuja-al-Dowlah, Afghan Minister in London.

24. Ghulam Jilani Khan, First Secretary in London.

25. Sayyid Akram Khan, Second Secretary in London.

26. Mirza Abdullah Khan, Second Secretary in London.

27. Muhammad Yunas Khan, Third Secretary in London.

Besides the personnels of the Afghan Legations abroad joined the Royal Party during the parts of their journey. The King spent well over seven months in travelling abroad. The tour itinerary was as follows[60] :

Departure from :	Kabul	:	November 29, 1927
	Chaman	:	December 10, 1927
	Karachi	:	December 11-12, 1927
	Bombay	:	December 14-17, 1927
	Egypt	:	December 26, 1927-January 3, 1928
	Italy	:	January 8-22, 1928

France	:	January 23 February 8, 1928
Belgium	:	February 8-11, 1928
Switzerland	:	February 12-19, 1928
Germany	:	February 20-March 7, 1928
England	:	March 13-April 5, 1928
France (unofficial)	:	April 6-9, 1928
Germany (unofficial)	:	April 10-28, 1928
Poland	:	April 29-May 2, 1928
Soviet Russia	:	May 3-18, 1928
Turkey	:	May 19, June 14, 1928
Iran	:	June 6-20, 1928
Arrival in Kabul	:	July 1, 1928

It was indeed a very costly affair and the risk involved in keeping away from the country for such a long time was obviously great. However, the outcome of journey were nine pacts ann protocols.[61]

1. Letto-Afghan	:	(February 1928)
2. Swiss-Afghan	:	(February 1928)
3. Japano-Afghan	:	(April, 1928)
4. Egypto-Afghan	:	(May 1928)
5. Turko-Afghan	:	(May 1928)
6. Perso-Afghan	:	(January 1928)
7. Perso-Afghan	:	(June 1928)
8. Finno-Afghan	:	(July 1928)
9. Liberian-Afghan	:	(1928)

Besides, negotiations were carried with China and

Hejaz. In Germany, Amanullah signed a preliminary Agreement giving concessions to the German and French firms to build railways in Afghanistan. This encouraged the Germans to make eco-political inroads in that country.

On May 2, 1928, the Royal Party of Afghanistan was received at the Soviet frontier by L.M. Karakhan, Assistant Commissioner for Foreign Affairs incharge of Eastern Question. Amanullah and his retinue arrived in Moscow on May 3, where the Royal Party was received by M.I. Kalinin, President of the Central Executive Committee; G.V. Chicherin, Commissar of Foreign Affairs; K. Voroshilov, Commissar of War, M.M. Latvinov, Assistant Commissar of Foreign Affairs; A. Mikoyan, Commissar of Finance and other Soviet officials. In his response to the welcome address of the Soviet Mufti, Sadruddinov, Amanullah riposted that the teachings of Islam were obfuscated by the conservative priests in regard to status of women.[62] He declared that polygamy and veils were the things of past and laid stress on dinkum indoctrinates of Islam. As in other countries, Amanullah donated one thousand pounds for the under-privileged people of Soviet Russia.

On his return to Afghanistan, Amanullah justified his trip on financial and political basis. In his speech of October 2, 1928, he adjudged the tour as a success costing 70,000 pounds. This amount was less than counter balanced by an income of 460,000 pounds in the form of gifts and grants. These figures did not include his purchases abroad, which were substantial. According to the German sources, these purchases amounted to 13-14 million marks in Italy and France, and about 6 million marks in Germany. According to the British reports, Amanullah received presents and made purchases during his foreign trip[63] are shown in Table.

Adducing his visit to Soviet Russia, Amanullah said, "From Poland, I proceeded to Moscow and met with the magnificent reception. Although they are Bolsheviks and do not like a King, yet they, for my sake, changed some

		Presents	Purchases
1.	Italy	1 Armored Car	1 Armoured Car
			2 Field Batteries
			4 Howitzer Batteries
			2 Pack Batteries
2.	France	1 Aeroplane	2 Field Batteries
			1 Pack Battery
			5 Light Tanks
			2 Ammunition Lorries
3.	Germany	1 Junker Aeroplane	2 Aeroplanes
4.	Poland	1 Aeroplane	—
5.	Soviet	2 Aeroplane	—
	Russia	2 Tanks	
		4 Tractors	

of their principles. I am exceedingly grateful to them. I met the Prime Minister and found the President an unassuming man. The War Minister and Mr. Chicherin paid me great respects, so much so that War Minister remained with me even on occasions when his presence was unnecessary. They wish to conclude a trade treaty, but I was too busy and sent for my Minister of Commerce to discuss the matter."[64]

During the Royal visit to Soviet Russia, three main desiderates revolved in the diplomatic negotiation.[65] The first was the conclusion of a trade treaty, which could not gain acceleration. Second was the construction of a direct road linking Kabul and Soviet territory, but the scarcity of resources made its execution difficult. The third was the conclusion of a four-corner pact between Turkey, Iran, Afghanistan and Soviet Russia on the basis of bilateral pacts already concluded between Soviet Russia and Turkey, Soviet Russia and Afghanistan, and, Turkey and Afghanistan. But Soviet Russia never wanted to make it a guarantee pact and no decision was arrived at.

Soviet-Afghan relations were provided solid foundations by Amanullah and these relations vigorously flourished to touch the last limits of friendship and mutual respect. These close ties washed off the British imperialism from Afghanistan and stood for liberation, progress and modernization of the Afghans.

References

1. Anuradha Sareen, *India and Afghanistan*, Delhi, 1981, p. 203.
2. W.K. Fraser-Tytler, *Afghanistan : A Study of Political Developments in Central Asia*, London, 1950, pp. 192-94.
3. George Grassmuch, ed., *Afghanistan : Some New Approaches*, Ann, Arbor, 1969, p. 269.
4. L.W. Adamec, *Afghanistan's Foreign Affairs to the Mid-Towentieth Century*, Arizona, 1974, p. 52.
5. Vartan Gregorian, *The Emergence of Modern Afghanistan*, California, 1969, p. 206.
6. A. Gromyko, ed., *History of Soviet Foreign Policy, 1919-45*, Moscow, 1969, p. 150, Ivar Spector, *The Soviet Union and the Muslim World, 1917-56*, U.S.A., 1956, pp. 54-55.
7. Ikbal Ali Shah, "Afghanistan in 1919", *Journal of Central Asian Society*, Vol. VII, 1920, Reprinted in 1963, pp. 3-10.
8. Jan. F. Triska and Robert M. Slusser, *The Theory, Law and Policy of Soviet Treaties*, *California*, 1962, p. 203.
9. V.I. Lenin, *The National Liberation Movement in the East*, Moscow, 1957, pp. 218-19.
10. Vartan Gergorian, *op. cit.*, pp. 238-39, Amalendu Guha, ed., *Central Asia*, Delhi, 1970, p. 264.
11. L. Mitrokhin, Lenin and the Revolutionaries of the East "—Interview with Mahendra Pratap, *Soviet Review*, Vol. XVII, No. 19, April 21, 1980, pp. 54-56.

    For the Fnglish translation of the concluding portion of *Bolshevism and the Islamic Nations*, See : G. Adhikari, ed., *Documents of the History of the Communist Party of India*, Vol. I, 1917-22, New Delhi, 1972, pp. 121-28.
13. For details : Leonid Mitrokhin, *Lenin and Indian Freedom Fighters*, New Delhi, 1988.
14. Sir Percy Sykes, "Afghanistan : The Present Position", *Journal of Royal Central Asian Society*, Vol. XXVII, April, 1940, pp. 149-52. J.G. Elliott, *The Frontier 1939-1947*, London, 1968; pp. 49-51. For detailed analysis, See : Mohammed Ali, *Afghanistan : The War of Independence 1919*, Kabul, 1960.
15. G. Adhikari, *op. cit.*, pp. 36-37, Amalendu Guha, *op. cit.*, p. 265. Vartan Gregorian, *op. cit.*, pp. 234-35.

16. L,w. Adamec, *op. cit.*, pp. 52-54.
17. *National Archives of India*, File No : 137-F/1920, Foreign Political Department.
18. A. Gromyko, *op. cit.*, p. 151. Ivar Spector, *op. cit.*, p. 54.
19. L.W. Adamec, *Afghanistan 1900-23*, Los Angles, 1967, pp. 143-44.
20. *Pravda*, December 18, 1955.
21. L.W. Adamec, *Afghanistan Foreign Affairs*, p. 54.
22. L.W. Adamec, *Afghanistan 1900-23*, pp. 142-43.
23. *Loc., cit*, p. 55.
24. Louis Dupree, *Afghanistan*, New Jersey, 1973, p. 443.
25. Y. Volkov, ed., *The Truth About Afghanistan*, Moscow, 1980, p. 22.
26. G. Adhikari, *op. cit.*, pp. 17, 113.
27. *National Archives of India*, File No. : 160-For, Sec./February, 1920, Foreign and Political Department.
28. L.W. Adamec, *Afghanistan's Foreign Affairs*, pp. 5-56.
29. Max Beloff, *The Foreign Policy of Soviet Russia*, 2 Volumes, London, 1955, Vol. II, p. 207.
30. L.W. Adamec, *Afghanistan 1900-1923*, p. 147.
31. L.W. Adamec, *Afghanistan's Foreign Affairs*, pp. 56-57.
32. Sir Percy Sykes, "Afghanistan : The Present Position", *JRCAS*, p. 153, Ivar Spector, *op. cit.*, p. 55
33. A. Gromyko, *op. cit.*, p. 152. Ivar Spector, *op. cit.*, p. 65.
34. E.H. Carr, *International Relations between the two World Wars 1919-39*, London, 1955, p. 74.
35. I.D. Ovayany, ed., *A Study of Soviet Foreign Policy*, Moscow, 1975, p. 95.
36. V.I. Lenin, *Collected Works*, Vol. 31, p. 491.
37. Alice Bird, "Afghanistan as an Independent Power", *Modern Review*, July 1921, p. 59.
38. Ved Pratap Vaidik, *Afghanistan Men Soviyat-Ameriki Pratispardha*, Hindi, Delhi, 1971, pp. 6-13.
39. Malcolm D. Kennedy, *A Short History of Communism in Asia*, London, 1925, p. 60.
40. Louis Dupree, *op. cit., p. 448.*
41. In the wake of First World War, Enver Pasha was driven out of Ottomon Empire. He took refuge first in Germany and then in Soviet Russia. He played a very important role in consolidating the Soviet Afghan relations. He also made Afghanistan to believe that Soviet Russia could help the pan-Islamic cause in the East. But in 1921, he became the leader of the Basmachies who were demanding separation of Bukhara and Khiva from the Soviet Union. He also tried to enlist the Basmachies for his pan-Turanian ideology. But he was defeated by the Soviets in June 1922 and died soon after. For more details, Vartan Gregorian, *op. cit.*, pp. 233-38.
42. Y. Volkov, *op. cit.*, pp. 24-26.

43. Jan M. Meijer, ed., *The Trotsky Papers 1917-22*, London, 1964, p. 673.
44. I.M. Reyser, *Afghanistan*, Moscow, 1929, pp. 205-07.
45. L.W. Adamec, *Afghanistan 1900-1923*, pp. 161-62.
46. A. Gromyko, *op. cit.*, p. 152.
47. For the details of British political measures and military operations in the border areas, W.K. Fraser Tytler, *Afghanistan*, Chapter 13.
48. G. Adhikar, *op. cit.*, pp. 110-11.
49. *Loc. cit.* pp. 204-06, Y. Volkov, *op. cit.*, p. 25. Ved Pratap Vaidik, *op. cit.*, p. 15.
50. *National Archives of India*, File No. : 203-F/1924, Foreign and Political Department.
51. L.W. Adamec, *Afghanistan's Affairs*, pp. 107-08.
52. *Loc. cit.*
53. *Izvestia*, December 23, 1923, Interview by Raskolnikov, Soviet Minister in Kabul, on Anglo-Afghan conflict.
54. X.J. Eudin and R.C. North, *Soviet Russia and the East 1920-1927*, California, 1964, p. 105.
55. *Aman-i-Afghan*, December 21, 1925.
56. *Aman-i-Afghan*, Februray 4 and March, 6, 1926.
57. A. Gromyko, *op. cit.*, p. 153.
58. *National Archives of India*, File No. : 502-F/1925, Foreign and Political Department.
59. *National Archives of India*, File Nos. : 46-F/1928 and 355-F/1928, Foreign and Political Department.
60. *National Archives of India*, File No. : 256-F/1928, Foreign and Political Department.
61. *National Archives of India*, File Nos. 84-N/1928, (Near East), 106-N/1928, (Near East), 119-N/1928 (Near East), 668-F/1932 (Frontier), Foreign Political Department.
62. *National Archives of India*, File No. : 46-F/1928, Foreign and Political Dpeartment.
63. *National Archives of India*, File No. : 256-F/1928, Foreign and Political Department.
64. L.W. Adamec, *Afghanistan's Foreign Affairs*, p. 136.
65. E.H. Carr, *Foundation of Planned Economy 1926-1929*, (A History of Soviet Russia), Vol. III, London, 1978, pp. 695-96.

3

At the Crossroads

Afghanistan became a slum of civil war in 1929. Most of the foreign diplomatic missions left Kabul, leaving behind Soviet mission rather uncomfortably.[1] Amanullah was forced to renounce the throne on 14th January and his brother, Inayatullah, became the new King.[2] But he was forced to abdicated only after three days. It was on January 18, 1929, that a bandit and highway man, Bach-i-Saqao, proclaimed himself King under the name of Habibullah. Great Britain was the first European power to grant the new regime "de facto" recognition.[3] On February 28, 1929, the British *Daily Mail* wrote that for coming into power Bach-i-Saqao was helped by Humphrys, the British Ambassador, with whom Bacha's envoy had a secret meeting before his attack on Kabul.[4] Soviet sources even connect Bacha with the British secret service.

With the change in Afghanistan, Soviet-Afghan relations were shattered. The diplomatic relations were not broken, but Soviets never granted any recognition to the bandit regime. In fact there developed a split in the decision-making bodies of Soviet Russia over the course of action to follow after the abdication of Amanullah.[5] The Comintern and the Soviet

Secret Police (O.G.P.U.) argued that Bacha was the leader of peasants and his revolt was social in nature. But the Commissariat of Foreign Affairs supported Amanullah. Soviet Press expressed the opinion that Bacha was restored in Afghanistan by Great Britain in order to establish close contacts with ex-Amir of Bukhara, Sayyid Alim, and the Basmachi leader, Ibrahim Beg.[6] The purpose was either to rekindle the Basmachi revolt in Soviet Central Asia or to provoke an aggressive move against Tadjikistan. According to the Soviet sources, Bacha aided and patronized anti-Soviet activities conducted from Afghan territory by the Basmachi bands.[7] It was also reported that about 2,000 Basmachi bandits stepped up their raids into Soviet territory from their harbourages in northern Afghanistan, to loot and terrorize the local population. Besides encouraging pro-Basmachi activities in Soviet Central Asia, Bacha-i-Saqao disseminated anti-Soviet propaganda among the Tadjiks. This compelled the Politburo of Soviet Russia to support Amanullah.

In 1928, a Soviet military force was sent to aid Amanullah in putting down the sedition.[8] But this could not save the throne of Amanullah. Again in 1929, Soviet Russia aided Ghulam Nabi, the Afghan Ambassador in Moscow, to mobilize and accelerate the pro-Amanullah sentiments in Afghanistan.[9] Ghulam Nabi crossed the Soviet-Afghan border and penetrated into Afghanistan. But his efforts were frustrated and he fled to the Soviet territory. However, the Soviet Press continued to be hostile to Bacha, attacked him and criticized his alliance with the British.[10] Bacha-i-Saqao's rule was considered as the darkness of middle ages and his alliance with the British as military adventure towards Soviet Russia. Even Iran was put on guard by Soviet Russia not to hope for annexation of Herat or partition of Afghanistan.[11] In its respond Iran reaffirmed her policy of non-intervention in the internal affairs of the neighbouring countries.

Great Britain accused the Soviet authorities for helping pro-Amanullah and anti-Bacha forces. It was alleged that being a socialist country, Soviet Russia was helping an autocratic King. It was on May 30, 1929, that *Habib-ul-Islam* carried a message of the Soviet President announcing neutrality and non-interference in the Afghan civil war.[12] With this ended the so-called Soviet intervention in the internal affairs of Afghanistan.

To counter the growing Soviet influence in Afghanistan, Great Britain granted "de facto" recognition to the bandit regime in that country but withdrew her diplomatic mission to avoid the alienation of Afghan tribes. The British authorities also tried to keep themselves open and non-committed.

Nadir Khan[13] was offered a major post by the Bacha-i-Saqao. After arriving in Peshawar, Nadir Khan received an offer from Amanullah also to join him in Kandahar. He, however, decided to launch an anti-Bacha campaign and proceeded to Khost in order to win the support of Afghan tribes.[14] On March 19, 1929, Nadir Khan asked Bacha to legitimise his claim to a National Jirga to be made up of all the Afghan chieftains. In reply, Bacha confiscated his property and imprisoned all the members of his family.[15] Even a prize of Rs. 40,000 and one gun for capturing Nadir alive or Rs. 30,000 and one gun for his head was announced.[16] An award of Rs. 10,000 and a gun for each of Nadir's brothers was also announced. However, Bacha-i-Saqao was defeated on October 6, 1929, and Nadir Khan entered Kabul on October 15. On October 16-17, 1929, Nadir Khan was proclaimed King of Afghanistan.[17] But his appointment to the Afghan throne became a subject of bitter controversy. Pro-Amanullah elements wanted the throne for Amanullah, who himself was interested to resume it.[18] The nationalist Afghans were fearing the accession of Nadir to the Afghan throne as a triumph for reactionary forces and an appeasement of the religious establishments.[19]

With the emergence of Nadir Khan, a new phase was opened in the foreign policy of Afghanistan. He was not in favour of any change in his foreign relations and declared that he would continue the relations with foreign countries according to the policy laid down by Amanullah, particularly with the neighbours.[20] Identical telegrams were sent to all countries, with which Afghanistan had relations, stating that freindly relations should continue on concrete foundations. Soviet Russia was the first country to recognize the Nadir Khan's regime in Afghanistan. In his reply to the Afghan message, L.M. Karakhan, Soviet Deputy Commissar for Foreign Affairs, assured Afghanistan that Soviet Russia had a desire to further develop the friendly relations for consolidation of Afghan independence and economic progress.[21] Leonide Stark, the Soviet Ambassador in Afghanistan, who had been absent throughout the period of civil war, now returned to Kabul. A cordial reception was given to him on his arrival in Kabul, including a salute of forty-one guns.

Soviet Russia did not explicity recognise Nadir Khan as King, but only referred to the relations between the two countries. In the early 1930, Afghanistan was not statisfied of its relations with Soviet Russia.[22] The demeanour of the Soviet authorities was not ascertained as dependable and reliable for the future. The British authorities received unconfirmed reports in 1930 about the arrival of 6,000 Soviet Muslim troops at Kushik with the ultimate aim of marching through Afghanistan to support the revolution in India.[23] But no confirmation was received and these reports were considered erroneous and mistaken.

Mutual suspicions developed between Soviet Russia and Afghanistan, disturbing the relations between the two countries. A secret understanding between Soviet Russia, Italy and Amanullah was reported in 1931, in which some Indians were also suspected to be involved.[24] Reports about the appointment of agents and Indo-Iran and Indo-Afghan frontiers also came in. It was during the period of civil war that Nadir Khan had a meeting with Richard Maconachie, a former British Counsellor in Kabul who was employed as British Political Agent in Kurram Valley. This caused some apprehension among the Soviets. However, Nadir Khan made a formal declaration of a policy of neutrality and friendship towards its neighbours.[25] But the British aid of 10,000 rifles, five million cartridges and about 180,000 sterling pounds indicated the British endorsement of Nadir's regime.[26] Some more loans were accepted from the west. Germany provided some 5,000 rifles and half a million cartridges.[27] These were supplemented with 5,000 rifles purchased from Britain and some 16,000 rifles with 1.8 million cartridges purchased from France. Soviet Russia condemned the Afghan government for accepting the loans and aids from Great Britain and other capitalist countries.[28] Nadir Khan justified these loans from the west on the grounds of imperative need.[29] He strongly denied that these loans and aids were accompanied with any condition or privilege.

In December, 1929, Soviet Foreign Minister, M.M. Litvinov, declared the Soviet desire to maintain friendly relations with Afghanistan based on mutual respect and cooperation.[30] Soviet Press was of the opinion that to counter the British colonialism and imperialism, Afghanistan should maintain close relatians with Soviet Russia, Iran and Turkey.[31] The principal problems constituting the Soviet-Afghan relations were :

1. Renegotiation of the Neutrality Pact of 1926;
2. Conclusion of a commercial treaty;
3. Extension of the Soviet airline concession;
4. Establishment of a frontier commission;
5. Conclusion of postal agreement;
6. Solution of refugee problem;
7. Eradication of the locusts by a bilateral campaign.

Nadir Khan was interested in constructing the friendly relations both with Soviet Russia and Great Britain. He never wanted that the Soviets should engage themselves in championing irredentist or revolutionary movements in northern Afghanistan. He did not also like the British to inspire tribal opposition against the Afghan monarchy. He had also the fear that either or both powers might advocate the cause of

Amanullah. As a precautionary step, Nadir Khan appointed his brother, Shah Wali, as envoy to London and sent another brother, Muhammad Aziz, to Moscow.[32]

The Red Shirt Movement[33] thrashed the British in India. They had the apprehensions that the Movement was communist oriented. The founder of the Movement, Abdul Gaffar Khan, blamed the British for the abdication of Amanullah and disturbances in Afghanistan. The Soviet Press also was enthusiastic in its support.[34] But soon the Soviet Press changed its attitude towards the movement and considered it as *Servants of Imperialism* instead of *Servants of God* or *Khudai Khidmatgaran* as the members of the Movement used to call themselves.[35] Analogously denounced by the Soviets and subversed by the British, Red Shirt Movement could not play any significant role in the foreign policy of Afghanistan. Even the King of Afghanistan, Nadir Khan, vengeanced the Movement because of Abdul Gaffar's close association with Amanullah.[36]

George Agabekov refer to an unestablished fact that when Nadir Khan applied for Soviet visa to enter Afghanistan in 1929, the Soviet authorities agreed on the condition that he would undertake the anti-British campaign.[37] Whatever may be the case, Nadir Khan was eager to establish close and friendly ties with Soviet Russia. But the Soviets were disturbed for his pro-British approach and considered him as a symptom of British imperialism.[38] French and British military assistance and financial credits to Afghanistan were considered as the shadows of anti-Soviet designs. In fact, Soviet Russia wanted to discourage Afghanistan from any tempting anti-Soviet ventures.

Soviet-Afghan Treaty of Neutrality and Non-aggression was signed on June 24, 1931, in which the provisions of the Treaty of 1926 were reconfirmed. By signing this Treaty, the rumours that the Soviet-Afghan relations had recently become so strained as to reach the breaking point after the murder of an Afghan Consul in Tashkent in November, 1930, were contradicted.[39] On July 6, 1931, in a speech to the National Council, Nadir Khan announced that Afghanistan would soon enter into negotiations with Soviet Russia regarding a commercial treaty and an agreement on the exchange of mail.[40] This revealed the Nadir Khan's desire to conciliate Soviet Russia.

In 1931, the pro-Amanullah agents were reported to be in constant touch with Amanullah.[41] The presence of Soviet agents in Herat was also reported, attempting to regain popularity for Amanullah among Gilzai, Durrani, Afridi, Shinwari, Gugiani, Mohamad Safi and Koh-i-Daman tribes by extensive pro-Amanullah and anti-Nadir propaganda.[42] Amanullah was known to have taken the opportunity of getting into touch with Soviet Foreign Office to acquire the Soviet help, at least benevolent neutrality. Amanullah intended to enter Afghanistan through Herat, where the Governor had assured him of his allegiance. But these British intellegence reports proved erroneous, wrong and incorrect.

During early 1930, refugees from Soviet Central Asia entered Afghanistan which put the Afghan government in trouble.[43] However, the situation was unravelled by settling the Muslims in northern Afghanistan, while the Europeans were sent to India and the Jews to China by way of the Wakhan Corridor. After sometime, the refugees in northern Afghanistan were transferred to the southern provinces for their anti-Soviet diligence. However, in June, 1930, Soviet troops violated the northern boundary of Afghanistan and penetrated near 40 miles southward in order to capture Ibrahim Beg, one of the last Basmachi leader, and to make the Afghan authorities deal firmly with anti-Soviet elements.[44] The British and American sources dyed the incident with different colour.[45] After strong opposition by Afghanistan and Great Britain, the Soviet troops had to go back. Finally in April, 1931, Ibrahim Beg was driven across the Soviet border, where he was captured. Northern Afghanistan was not to be tolerated as a pasture for anti-Soviet, pan-Islamic and pan-Turkic activities.

In 1932, Soviet troops were reported increasing along the whole length of the frontier from the Caspian to the Chinese border, to stop the constant emigration that had been going on across the border and to deal with Basmachi raids which were particularly troublesome in the Pamirs and Merv districts.[46] Ait Merek was the notorious Basmachi leader who scuppered several Soviet posts during the winter months, including the important one of Irkishtan on the Sinkiang border. But the strengthening of the Soviet frontier guards and troop movements, in connection with operations against the Basmachies or in association with normal training, became the cause of Afghan anxiety. To wash off the Afghan anxiety, an Agreement was reached between the two countries for the settlement of frontier disputes.[47] But no important incident was reported which required any immediate attention of the Soviet-Afghan Commissars. Afghanistan also favoured the Soviet view at Disarmament Conference.[48] This was the first time in the history of Soviet-Afghan relations since 1919 that both countries articulately spoke on international situation.

According to the British secret reports, about 80 Hazaras and Afghans were collected by Soviet Intelligence Agents and sent to Tirmiz to support the cause of Amanullah in December, 1932.[49] In January, 1933, reports came that one of the secretaries of Afghan Embassy in Moscow had put to death his "Russian wife" after recognising her as an agent of Soviet Intelligence.[50] Meanwhile a rumour with doubtful accuracy spread in Merv that Amanullah had arrived in Moscow under a false passport and that his son was in Tashkent.[51] Ghulam Rasool Khan, brother of Ghulam Nabi Khan, was said to have arrived in Merv from Tashkent, recruited about 50 Hazaras and Afghans, and proceeded to Kushk. But, as earlier, these reports were also found stumble and transient.

Soviet-Afghan relations flourished with the signing of Convention for the Definition of Aggression by the plenipotentiaries of Afghanistan, Estonia, Latvia, Iran, Poland, Rumania, Turkey and Soviet Russia on June 3, 1933, at London. The Convention was identical in its substance with the *definition of aggression adopted* by the Security Committee of the Disarmament Conference. The Afghans considered the Convention as an assurance of security offered by Soviet Russia.[52]

The Soviets had very correctly formed the opinion that sovereignty of Afghanistan was facing a grave threat as the British wanted to dominate the country in the name of defence and security.[53] Nadir Khan, who was interested in the socio-economic and political integration of his country, never showed any preference to great Britain or Soviet Russia. He was interested to develop the close relations with France, Italy, Germany, Japan and the United States. For the defence of his northern boundary, Nadir Khan adopted a policy of non-intervention in Soviet Central Asia. His policy of neutrality was painful both for the Soviet and the British. The Soviet proposals to establish commercial missions at various centres in Afghanistan were rejected. Even no British national was employed in any capacity throughout the country.

Afghan aviation was under the Soviet influence during the times of Amanullah. Most of the pilots and maintenance personnel were provided by Soviet Russia. Since 1927, air service existed on regular schedule between the two countries from Tirmiz, on the Soviet border, to Kabul. Nadir Khan intended to extend a flight of German Junkers Airlines Company from Iran to Afghanistan. But the negotiations failed in 1932 because the Junkers insisted on termination of Soviet Airline Service, which was not acceptable to the Afghans. It was only in 1937 that Lufthansa started the weekly service between Berlin and Kabul, first regular air link between Europe and Afghanistan.[54] Soviet pilots and maintenance personnel remained in Afghanistan during the early months of Nadir Khan's reign, but were withdrawn from Afghan Air Force when the Afghans, who were trained in Soviet Russia, Italy and France formed the nucleus of the new Afghan Air Force.

The Afghans were perturbed with the Carnivorous

British imperialism. Anti-British propaganda increased in Afghanistan. On June 6, 1933, Muhammad Aziz, brother of the King and Afghan minister in Berlin, was assassinated by an Afghan student as a protest against the predominance of British influence in Afghanistan.[55] The relations between Afghanistan and Germany got disturbed owing to the dilatoriness of the Germans in deciding the fate of the murderer of Muhammad Aziz. In this state of confusion, Nadir Khan was himself shot dead by the natural son of Ghulam Nabi, on November 8, 1933, during a school prize-giving function in the grounds of Dilkusha Palace.[56] After the assassination of Nadir Khan, his nineteen-year old son Zahir Khan ascended the throne.

With the accession of Zahir Khan to the Afghan throne, the real power was laid in the hands of his paternal uncle, the Afghan Bismark-Mahammed Hasim Khan, who assumed the complete control of the country's domestic and foreign policies as Prime Minister. On 14th November, 1933, Soviet Russia granted the official recognition to Zahir Shah's government.[57]

Hashim Khan was anxious to maintain equilibrium between the nearest neighbours of Afghanistan to avoid political intrication. He turned to Central Europe, especially to Germany, for financial credits and assistance in expertise. By 1935, the German Afghan relations had improved as the assassin of Muhammad Aziz was tried and executed. Taking it as an opportunity to grind her axe in Central Asia, Germany started its penetration into the socio-economic and political affairs of Afghanistan.

To improve the traditional relations with Soviet Russia, Hashim Khan declared that the Basmachies and other emigre elements from Central Asia would not be allowed to engage themselves in anti-Soviet activities. The Afghan religious establishments were directed to stop any moral support to the Basmachi bands and other emigre elements. Some of the anti-Soviet leaders were forced to migrate to Turkey or

Europe. To conciliate Soviet Russia, Afghanistan did not join the league of Nations until 1934, when at last Soviet Russia too decided to do the same. Soviet Foreign Minister, Maksim Maksimovich Litvinov, emanated a very impressive statements on the entry of Afghanistan into the league of Nations, September 25, 1934, advocating more close ties between the two countries.[58] Soviet Russia was adequately satisfied with the entry of Afghanistan into the League.[59]

On November 19, 1930, Treaty of Friendship was signed between Japan and Afghanistan.[60] But it was only in November, 1935, that Japan established its Legation in Afghanistan, perhaps to watch the developments in Soviet Russia. Japan obviously wanted to use Afghanistan as a look-out post on events across the Oxus. It seemed likely that before long the question of the hegemony of eastern Asia would have to be decided between the Soviets and the Japanese. A Japanese mission was also a useful counter-balance to the British imperialism in Afghanistan. But Afghanistan did not care much for a capitalist country-Japan.

Great Britain constantly tried to injure Soviet-Afghan relations for her own imperialist designs.[61] It was because of the continuous anti-Soviet propaganda by the British that in 1936 Afghan Foreign Minister, Faiz Muhammad, requested the British Indian authorities to make a search for the papers pertaining to Soviet Afghan frontier.[62] However, Hashim Khan strictly followed the primary principles of Soviet-Afghan Treaty of Neutrality and non-Aggression, signed in 1931.[63] In March 1936, Afghan Foreign Minister visited Soviet Russia where a cordial reception was granted to him.[64] A protocol was signed between the two countries on March 29, 1936, renewing and extending the Soviet-Afghan Treaty of 1931 till 1946. The reaction of Germany, which by this time had developed as third power in Afghanistan, to the Soviet-Afghan Protocol was that of displeasure and perplexity. The Afghan War Minister, Shah Muhmmad Khan, visited Moscow in September 1936, which vigorously strengthened the relations between the two countries.[65]

In July 1937, an Alliance between Iran, Iraq, Turkey and Afghanistan was concluded, known as the Saadabad Pact.[66] The negotiations for this Pact had been initiated in 1934. Soviet Russia, which had non-aggression and other pacts with Turkey and Afghanistan, considered the Saadabad Pact as an extension of collective security to help stabilization of peace and political coordination in the region.[67] Great Britain and Germany also hailed the Pact.[68] However, Italy considered it as an instrument of British imperialism in the Middle East.[69] In fact, Saadabad Pact was concluded with the tacit approval or even with the active encouragement of Soviet Russia and Great Britain.[70] Some considered it as a triumph for Soviet diplomacy to limit the power of Great Britain in the region, while others viewed it as an attempt by the British to safeguard their political and economic interests in the region against the Soviet self-assertion and Italian expansion.[71]

The United States of America also began to take interest in Afghanistan by this time. While Nadir Khan was not granted any recognition by the United States, King Zahir Khan was granted the same by a letter dated August 21, 1935.[72] An Afghan-American Treaty was signed on March 26, 1936, in Paris. Symptoms of the U.S. cannibalism in Afghanistan were gradually developing. To be more clear, the U.S. imperialism was barbarously preparing to open its claws to replace the carnivorous British colonialism and capitalism.

Relations between Soviet Russia, Iran, Afghanistan and Turkey were fluctuating in 1938. Germany consolidated and strengthened its position in Afghanistan. There were reports that during a meeting with the Soviet Ambassador in Kabul, his Japanese counterpart asked him to collect intelligence reports for Japan.[73] This perplexed the Soviet authorities and compelled the Soviet Press to adopt hostile approach. The Afghan Ambassador in Moscow was also blamed for spreading the rumours of Soviet-Japanese War. These developments disturbed the traditional Soviet-Afghan relations for some time.

Great Britain was perturbed over the establishment of Soviet Consulates in Afghanistan since 1921.[74] However, to remove the fears of interference in each others internal affairs, both Soviet Russia and Afghanistan agreed to close down their respective Consulates in Mazar-i-Sharif and Tashkent.[75] This provided some relief to the British.

References

1. E.H. Carr, *Foundation of Planned Economy 1926-29*, (A History of Soviet Russia), Vol. III, London, 1978, p. 697.
2. Abdual Qadir Khan, "The Outlook in Afghanistan", *Journal of Royal Central Asian Society*, Vol. 19, 1932, pp. 463-66. W.K. Fryser-Tytler, *Afghanistan*, London, 1950, pp. 212-17. For detailed Study : Ikbal Ali Shah, *Tragedy of Amanullah*, London, 1914. Ronald Violed, *Ex-King of Afghanistan*, London, 1032. Muhammad Ali, *Progressive Afghanistan, Lahore, 1933.*
3. Abdul Qadir Khan, "The Outlook in Afghanistan;', *JRCAS*, p. 466.
4. Y. Volkov, *The Troth About Afghanistan*, Moscow, 1980, p. 26. P.N. Fedoseyev, *Afghanistan : Past and Present* Moscow, 1981, pp. 154-55.
5. Vartan Gregorian, *The Emergence of Modern Afghanistan*, California, 1969, pp. 278-79.
6. *Pravda*, May 10, 1929. *Izvestia*, May, 10, 1929.
7. Y. Volkov, *op. cit.*, p. 27.
8. Robert G. Wesson, *Soviet Foreign Policy in Perspective*, USA, 1969, p. 256.
9. *Pravda*, May 8, 1929, Abdul Qadir Khan, "Afghanistan since the Revolution", *Journal of Central Asian Society*, Vol. 17, 1930, p. 322. Joseph Castagne, "Soviet Imperialism in Afghanistan", *Foreign Affairs*, July 1935, p. 702.
10. *Zaria Vostoka*, (Tiflis), February 17, 1929, *Izvestia*, February 26-28 1929. Mustapha Chokaiev, "The Bolsheviks and Afghanistan", *Asiatic Review*, July 1929, p. 510, and "The situation in Afghanistan", *Asiatic Review*, 1930, p. 326.
11. *Zaria Vostoka* (Tiflis), April 18, 1929, *Pravda*, April 25, 1929.
12. *National Archives af India*, File No. : 190-F/1929, Foreign and Political Department.
13. Born in 1813, Nadir Khan was third cousin of Amanullah and the brother of the second wife of Amir Habibullah (father of Amanullah). He worked as Commander-in-Chief of Amanullah from May 1919 to September 1922. In August 1924, he was appointed as

Afghan Minister to France. In 1926, he resigned from the post because of difference with Amanullah and also owing to his own ill health.

14. Mustapha Chokaiev, "The Situation in Afghanistan", *Asitatic Review*, April 1930, p. 328.
15. N.N. Ghosh, "The Afghan Civil War 1928-29", *The Modern Review*, Februray, 1930, p. 181.
16. *Pioneer*, April 24, 1929.
17. George Grassmuck, ed., *Afghanistan : Some New Approaches*, Michigam, 1969, p. 272.
18. *Pioneer*, October 18-19, 1928. *Izvestia*, July 24, 1930. N.N. Ghosh, *op. cit.*, p. 184.
19. Arnold Fletcher, "Afghanistan : Highway of Conquest", *Current History*, January, 1950, pp. 221-22.
20. Muhammad Ali, *Progressive Afghanistan*, Lahore, 1933, pp. 173-174.
21. *Izvestia*, October 20, 1929.
22. *National Archives of India*, File Nos. : 540-F/1931 and 137-F/1931, Foreign and Political Department.
23. *National Archives of India*, File No. 216-F/1930, Foreign and Political Department.
24. *National Archives of India*, File No. 183-F/1931, Foreign and Political Department.
25. *Islah*, July 8, 1931.
26. W.K. Fraser-Tytler, *Afghanistan*, London, 1950, p. 231. Ved Pratap Vaidik, *Afghanistan Men Soviyat-Ameriki Pratispardha*, Hindi, Delhi, 1973, p. 26. Vartan Gregorian, *op. cit.*, p. 297. Also see *Daily Telegraph*, November 8, 1933.
27. Muhammad Ali, *op. cit.*, pp. 212-14.
28. Joseph Castagne, *op. cit.*, p. 702.
29. *Islah*, July 8, 1931. Ikbal Ali Shah, *Modern Afghanistan*, London, 1938, pp. 235-36.
30. Jain Degras, ed , *Soviet Documents on Foreign Policy*, 2 Volumes, London, 1951, Vol. II, pp. 430-31.
31. Joseph Castagne, *op. cit.*, pp. 702-06.
32. Louis Fischer, *Soviets in World Affairs*, London, 1930, Vol. II, p. 793.
33. Founded in 1921, The Organisation was known as *Society of Afghan, Reformation*, and later on as *Afghan Youth League*. After 1929-30, it was known as *Central Afghan Jirga*. The founder of this movement was Abdul Ghaffar Khan (1890-1988), a devotee of Amanullah and inspired by non-violence of Mahatma Gandhi.
34. *Pravada*, July 4, 1931. *Zaria Vostoka*, July, 16, 1931.
35. *Zaria Vostoka*, September 10, 1931.
36. Krishnalal Shridharani, "The Frontier Gandhi" *Asia*, September 1941, p. 469.

37. George Agabekov, *OGPU, The Russian Secret Terror*, New York, 1931, pp. 169-70.
38. *Zaria Vostoka*, July 21, September 14 and 21, 1930, December 27, 1931.
39. *Frankfurter Zeitung*, November, 21, 1930.
40. *National Archives of India*, File No. 566-F/1932, Foreign aad Political Department.
41. *National Archives of India*, File No. 617-F/1931, Foreign and Political Department.
42. *Ibid.*
43. Joseph Castagne, *op. cit.*, p. 703.
44. W.K. Fraser-Tytler, *Afghanistan*, pp. 229-30.
45. Donald N. Wilber, "Afghanistan, Independent and Encircled", *Foreign Affairs*, New York, April 1953, p. 490. R.T. Stewart, *Fire in Afghanistan*, New York, 1973, pp. 560-562. See also Joseph Castagne, *op. cit.*
46. *National Archives of India*, File No. 860-F/1932, Foreign and Political Department.
47. Jane Degras, *op. cit*, pp. 535-41.
48. Max Beloff, *The Foreign Policy of Soviet Russia 1929-41*, Vol. II, London, 1955, pp. 51-52
49. *National Archives of India*, File No. 326-F/1933, Foreign and Political Department.
50. *National Archives of India*, File No. 107/F/1933, Foreign and Political Department.
51. *Loc. cit.*
52. *National Archives of India*, File No. 402-X/1933, External Department.
53. *Zaria Vostoka*, January 28, 1931.
54. George Grassmuck, *op. cit.*, p. 274.
55. W.K Fraser-Tytler, *Afghanistan*, P. 240.
56. *Ibid.*, p. 241.
57. *Izvestia*, November 18, 1933.
58. *Izvestia*, September 27, 1934.
59. Abdul Qadir Khan, "Afghanistan in 1934", *Journal of Royal Central Asian Society*, Vol. 22, April, 1935, pp. 214-16.
60. W.K. Fraser-Tytler, *Afghanistan*, p. 252.
61. Sir Percy Sykes, "Afghanistan, The Present Position", *Journal of Royal Central Asian Society*, Vol. 27, April, 1949, pp. 161-62.
62. *National Archives of India*, File No. 576-F/1936, Foreign and Political Department.
63. Donald N. Wilber, Ed., *Afghanistan*, New Haven, 1956, p. 151.
64. *Izvestia*, March, 14, 1936.
65. *Izvestia*, September 27, 1936.
66. *League of Nations*, Treaty Series, Vol. 164, 1935-36, pp. 345-49.
67. *Izvestia*, July 10, 1937.

68. *The Times*, July 19, 1939.
69. George E. Kirk, Ed.,"The Middle East in the War 1939-46", *Survey of International Affairs*, Oxford, 1952, p. 490.
70. Sir Percy Sykes, *A History of Afghanistan*, 2 Volumes, London, 1940, Vol. II, p. 344.
71. Bernard Lewis, *Turkey Today*, London, pp. 68-77.
72. Ved Pratap Vaidic, *op. cit.*, pp. 31-38.
73. *Ibid.*, p. 37.
74. *National Archives of India*, File No. 60-F/1929, Foreign and Political Department.
75. *Islah*, April 25, 1938.

4

Road to Crisis

On the eve of the Second World War, Afghanistan's foreign policy was based on determination to cultivate friendly relations with all foreign countries and to maintain pre-War economic policy.[1] The Soviet-Afghan relations were overshadowed by the Afghan fears that Soviet Russia might take military action against India and for this purpose would also invade Afghanistan.[2] The people of Afghanistan also perceived that Soviet Russia had begun to treat her consular offices as springboards for dealing with Afghan Frontier Tribes to encourage them for taking hostile measures against India. But these painful dreads were allayed when it was announced that the Soviet Consulates in Herat, Mazar-i-Sharif and Maimana, and the Afghan Consular Offices in Tashkent and Merv were to be closed.[3]

On August 23, 1939 the Soviet German Non-Aggression Treaty was concluded. Germany attacked Poland on September Ist, with which broke the Second World War. In December, Italian Press reported the activities of Soviet troops on the Afghan border.[4] The Afghan troops were also reported being sent to Soviet frontiers. British troops were also said of having started a march towards the Soviet frontiers.[5] But these reports proved nothing more than German propaganda in order to get Soviet Russia into the Axis camp.

Afghanistan, which had entered into commercial relations with Germany in 1935-36, was largely dependent on German credits for its welfare and development schemes.[6] Italian engineers were entrusted the execution of Afghanistan's big irrigation schemes, the building of dykes, roads and bridges, technical supervision of the arsenal and the instruction in the artillery school. This heavy dependence of Afghanistan on the Axis nations for financial and technical assistance in its economic development placed it in a precarious position.[7] Such dependence was naturally objectionable to Soviet Russia and Great Britain. In 1939, Soviet Russia raised the question of the Oxus river boundary with Afghanistan by claiming that the left bank of the river was the boundary between the two countries—Soviet Russia and Afghanistan.[8] The Afghans were disturbed by the Soviet claim. Soviet-German Agreement of August 1939 was considered ambiguous by the Afghans. British agents even spread the rumours that Soviet Russia and Germany want to liquidate Afghanistan.

The economic and foreign policies of Afghanistan were jolted by the conclusion of Soviet-German Agreement and the outbreak of Second World War. Afghanistan tried its best to maintain neutrality, but the war badly disturbed its economic development. The effect of the war was gradually to cut off Afghanistan in an increasing degree from her European markets and other sources of supply. There was considerable dislocation of trade in the country. Because of the Axis operations in the sea, export of Karakul to London became difficult and New York emerged as the principal market of Afghan Karakul.[9] Welfare schemes, development projects and military requirements in Afghanistan also suffered. Textile mills were half finished, hydro-electric installations lacked essential parts and guns needed ammunition.[10] Much of the material ordered from Czechoslovakia and Germany was still to come. The severance of relations with Germany was unfortunate for Afghanistan.

The Afghans saw their independence in danger and a threat was felt that their territory might become a battlefield for European diplomacy. Following the traditional guidelines, Afghanistan declared neutrality in the War. The Axis nations tried to force Afghanistan to give up its policy of neutrality, but their efforts failed.[11] Irritated by the neutrality of Hashim Khan, the Germans tried to secure the cooperation of Amanullah, ex-King of Afghanistan, and wanted to restore him to the throne.[12] But Soviet Russia refused to participate in the conspiracy. Then the Germans made attempts to win over the support from other sources. It was Abdul Majid Zabuli, Afghan Minister of Economy and President of the National Bank, who agreed to mobilize the anti-British tribal resistance in the North-West Frontier Province to prevent Indian forces being sent to the Mediterranean.[13] But in the return Zabuli demanded that the Germans were not to upset the delicate balance of power between Great Britain and Soviet Russia in Afghanistan, the Germans were to guarantee the Afghan territory the aggression of Soviet Russia and were to supply Afghanistan with heavy armaments including airplanes, tanks and artillery.

Germany repeatedly compelled Soviet Russia to move into Afghanistan to confuse the British in India.[14] But the Soviets were not interested in territorial expansion at the cost of Afghan friendship. The Germany Envoy in Kabul confidently announced in early 1940 that Hitler would be in London by August. He offered Afghanistan the restoration of the Durrani Empire[15]—including Baluchistan, Sind, Kashmir, Western Punjab together with the Port of Karachi.[16] A study of Soviet sources reveal that the Germans even prompted Afghanistan to annex the whole of Central Asia.[17] By this time Germany also managed to spread its influence among the tribes in the south of Afghanistan and in the north-western border areas.

Afghanistan tried to maintain cordial political and economic relations with the belligerent powers. Yet Soviet-Afghan relations remained somewhat tense.[18] Even Soviet troops were reportedly stationed in large numbers along the Afghan border. However after the conclusion of the Trade Agreement on July 29, 1940, between Bank-i-Milli and Savafgantory for one year, the relations between the two countries improved.[19]. Soviet-Afghan trade continued and was not allowed to cease till 1941. In fact, Afghan trade with Axis nations had diminished almost to the vanishing point, and Afghanistan had mainly to depend on Soviet Russia and British India.

In 1941, Iraq was carrying on the anti-British nationalist campaign.[20] Germany wanted to secure the support of Afghanistan for this campaign. But Afghanistan sagaciously decided to maintain neutrality.[21] However, Iraq asked Afghanistan to take up its cause under the Saadabad Pact and to call a *Jihad* (Holy war) against Great Britain. But Afghanistan never considered the request seriously, as there was no such move before signing the Saadabad Pact. In fact, Afghanistan was not in favour of adopting a rival and hostile attitude towards Great Britain or Soviet Russia. The Afghans were well aware of their strategic position and delicate relationship with British India and Soviet Russia. King Zahir Shah prudently proclaimed the Act of Neutrality which was approved by the Afghan Parliament.[22]

Germany attracted Soviet Russia on June 22, 1941.[23] The German attack not only caused terror in Soviet Russia, but also made the Soviet-Afghan relations to suffer. Even the commercial relations between two countries ceased to exist during 1942-47. Axis nations fomented the anti-Soviet feelings in Afghanistan. The anti-Soviet broadcast in Pushtu and Dari were organized in Berlin and Rome. The German authorities even thought of invading Afghanistan. Halder, Chief of the German General Staff, was told by Hitler to submit the information needed for military operations in Afghanistan and other Asian countries.[24]

From September 29—October 1, 1941, Moscow Conference was held between Soviet Russia, Great Britain and United States of America. On Junuary, 1, 1942, a Declaration was signed in Washington by 26 states, providing for joint resistance to the Tripartite Pact States—Germany, Italy and in Japan. The Treaty of Alliance was signed on May 26, 1942, in London between Soviet Russia and Great Britain against Germany and her associates. The Treaty also provided for cooperation and mutual assistance even after the war. In this way, two traditional rivals in Asia came close to each other.

Germany tried to establish contacts with the Russian white Emigres and still existing Basmachi leaders. The purpose was to conduct subversive activities against Soviet Russia. The Germans employed in Afghanistan distributed anti-Soviet literature and spread slanderous rumours to spoil the Soviet image in that country. Even terrorist bands were organized by the German agents in Afghanistan to penetrate into Soviet Central Asia, carry on subversive activities there and attack the Soviet border posts.[25] Von Hentig, German Minister in Afghanistan, was instructed to coordinate the activities of German teachers, officers, engineers and doctors, who had succeeded in penetrating the government apparatus and particular branches of the Afghan economy, to establish contacts with the Afghan nationalists. The Germans wanted to coordinate the frontier tribes and their leaders in order to use them against the Afghan government. With these developments, Soviet Russia became eager to demand for the immediate expulsion of "Fascist Intelligence Agents" (Germans, Italians and Japanese) from Afghanistan.

By this time, the United States was getting interested in Afghanistan. The U.S. Minister in Kabul was of opinion that the Afghans fear a Soviet attack after the World War. The Afghan Minister in Washington discussed with U.S. Foreign Secretary the issues concerning the grabbing of the territory by Russia in 1884 and other frontier problems.[26] This reveals the fact that Afghanistan was also eager to establish close relations with the United States.

A brief outburst on the Indo-Afghan frontier, which was said to have been engineered by the Italians, was quickly suppressed in 1941.[27] The Italians were reportedly trying to establish contacts with Haji Mirza Ali (Fakir of Ipi), an anti-British tribal leader of Waziristan during 1937-1941.[28] In July 1941, Afghan border guards fired at two Germans who tried to cross the border and join the Haji Mirza across the Indian frontiers.[29] One of the two Germans was killed and the other wounded. Hashim Khan conveyed his regret to the Germans on this incident, but he demanded that Afghanistan's neutrality be observed.

Germans and Italian activities in Afghanistan were becoming unbearable for the British and the Soviets. Earlier Soviet Russia and Great Britain had separately expressed their concern over the presence of the Axis nationals in Afghanistan. In October, 1941, similar notes were sent to Afghan Government by Soviet Russia and Great Britain demanding the immediate ouster of the Axis nationals.[30] On October 11, 1941, the Soviet Ambassador in Afghanistan expressed grievance over the role played by the Axis nationals in disturbing the friendly relations between the two countries.[31] The Soviets also alleged that terrorist groups organized by German commercial travellers had made armed raids into the Turkmen, Tadjik and Uzbek Soviet Republics. In October, 1941, Soviet Russia and Great Britain demanded the expulsion of the Axis nationals from Afghanistan within one month. However, in respect of the Afghan sovereignty, they conceded that the staff of Axis nations' legations should remain. The Soviets justified their demand on the basis of the Soviet-Afghan Treaty of 1931, which stated that in the case of war with a third power, both the countries would maintain strict neutrality and not permit its territory to be used by third power to the injury of other.

To avoid experiencing the same fate as that of Iran, Afghanistan agreed to expel the Axis nationals. By the end of October, 1941, 206 Axis nationals, including women and children, had left for Europe via Iran and Turkey.[32] The Afghan Government regarded the action taken as part of its neutral policy.[33] However, the Afghan reaction to this constrain of Allies was apprehension, bitterness and public outcry. Afghans saw this demand as a transgression of their sovereign rights. In fact, Afghanistan had maintained its neutrality from the beginnings, when Great Britain stood alone.

National Assembly (Loe Jirga) of Afghanistan was summoned to reveiw the situation in the country.[34] It reaffirmed the sovereignty and neutrality of Afghanistan; and refused to allow the occupation of any part of Afghanistan or the concession of land or air routes in or through the country. These moves were primarily directed against Soviet Russia and Great Britain.

With the expulsion of the Axis nationals from Afghanistan, the German expectations and desire that the Afghans would take up arms on their side were washed off. No doubt, Afghanistan stressed her friendly feeling towards Germany several times; but it never wanted to take any hostile step against Soviet Russia and Great Britain, now allies.

Afghanistan escaped the fate of Iran during the war, but she paid a high price for it. Her economy was dislocated and her projects for development were abandoned. Market for Afghan exports was reduced because the Allied occupation of Iran had cut off the trade route to Afghanistan. Afghanistan also feared an attack from Germany. However, Afghanistan was relieved of its anxiety when tide of war turned in favour of the Allies.

In 1942, Saadabad Pact had been automatically renewed for another five years.[35] The renewal of the Pact revealed the desire of the Middle Eastern countries to continue friendly collaboration despite chaos and confusion created by war.

If Afghanistan had shown some support to the Axis nationals, the results of Second World War would have been something different. Soviet Russia acknowledged the cooperation provided by Afghanistan and accorded it every assistance to fill the economic vacuume created by War. In the political field, a settlement of the vexed Oxus Frontier question with Soviet Russia was the important event to be decided. On June 13, 1946, a Soviet-Afghan Frontier Treaty was signed, with that started a new era of mutual respect, cooperation and co-existance in the traditional relations of two great countries.

References

1. W.K. Fraser-Tytler, "Afghanistan: A Brief Description," *Journal of Royal Central Asian Society*, 1942, p. 173.
2. L.W. Adamec, *Afghanistan's Foreign Affairs to the mid-twentieth century*, p. 244.
3. *Islah*, March 31, 1938, *National Archives of India*, File No. 244-F/1938, Foreign and Political Department.
4. Ved Pratap Vaidik, *Afghanistan Men Soviyat-Ameriki Pratispardha*, p. 30.
5. *New York Times*, December, 28, 1939
6. W.K. Fraser-Tytler, "Afghanistan: A Brief Description," *JKCAS*, p. 173.
7. Vartan Gregorian, *The Emergence of Modern Afghanistan*, p. 382.
8. *National Archives of India*, File No. 46-F/1939, Foreign and Political Department.
9. Amalendu Guha, Ed., *Central Asia*, p. 271.
10. W.K. Fraser-Tytler, "The expulsion of Axis Nationals from Afghanistan," *Survey of International Affairs*, 1939-1946, London, 1952, p. 142.
11. *Y*. Volkov, Ed., *The Truth About Afghanistan*, p. 27.
12. Lukaz Hirszowics, *The Third Reich and the Arab East*, London, 1966, pp. 70-71.
13. Vartan Gregorian, *op. cit.*, p. 386.
14. R.J. Sontag and J.S. Beddie, Eds., *Nazi-Soviet Relations 1939-1941*, Washington, 1948, p. 250.
15. Ahmed Shah Abdali or Durrani, the first king of unified Afghanistan, had expanded his dominions up to northern India and extended the Afghan sovereignty from Indus to Oxus.
16. W.K. Fraser-Tytler, "The Expulsion of Axis Nationals from Afghanistan," *Survey*, p. 143.
17. Y. Volkov, *op. cit.*, p. 28,
18. L.W. Adamec, *Afghanistan's Foreign Affairs*, p. 245.
19. David J. Dallin, *Soviet Russia's Foreign Policy 1936-1942*, New Heven, 1942, p. 421.

20. Vartan Gregorian, *op. cit.*, pp. 386-87.
21. W.K. Fraser-Tytler, "The Expulsion of Axis Nationals from Afghanistan," *Survey*, p. 144.
22. For the text and approval of the Afghan Naturality Act, See, *Kaboul Almanch 1939-1940*, pp. 47, 432-33. For its reaffirmation, see: *The Times*, July, 3, 1942.
23. Ken Russell, Tr., *History of the U.S.S.R.*, 3 Volumes, Moscow, 1977, Vol. III, p. 293.
24. Y. Volkov, *op cit.*, p. 28.
25. *Ibid.*
26. Ved Pratap Vaidik, *op. cit.*, pp. 42-43.
27. W.K. Fraser-Tytler, *Afghanistan*, p. 253.
28. Vartan Gregorian, *op. cit.*, p. 388.
29. W.K. Fraser-Tytler, "Afghanistan: A Brief Description", *JRCAS*, p. 174.
30. W.K. Fraser-Tytler, *Afghanistan*, pp. 254-55. *The Times*, October 21, 1941.
31. W.K. Fraser-Tytler, "The Expulsion of Axis Nationals from Afghanistan", *Survey*, pp. 145-46.
32. *Ibid.*
33. *The Times*, October 25, 1941.
34. *Kaboul Almanch 1941-1942*, pp. 280-85.
35. *The Times*, December 28, 1942.

5

Trade and Commerce

With the beginning of 20th century, Afghanistan inherited the age old power rivalry, which made its position like that of a wrecked boat in a vast stormy ocean tossed here and there and likely to be crashed against the rocks of imperialism at any movement. Czarist Russia and imperial Britain reduced it to a more skeleton between their Asian dominions.

Russian commercial advances in Central Asia had exposed Afghanistan to that country. It was with the declaration of Anglo-Russian Convention of 1907 that Russia agreed to retract its interference in the Afghan affairs provided that her economic interests were guaranteed, in the northern part of Afghanistan. During 1901-13, much of the Afghan trade was carried on with British India. However, Russo-Afghan trade continued even during the World War I. With the revolution of 1917, Russia became socialist and began to enlist the support of other nations for its newly established Bolshevik regime. The emergence of vigorous Amanullah on the Afghan throne proved disastrous for British imperialism, and Soviet-Afghan friendship gained a solid base. However, due to the prevailing conditions in Russia and Afghanistan during 1918-23, the Russo-Afghanistan trade remained suspended.

The Soviet-Afghan Agreement of 1921 provided the general terms for the future course of commercial and political relations. This Agreement stipulated a dynamic growth to Soviet-Afghan trade after 1923. Soviet Russia even sacrificed the state monopoly in foreign trade for sometime and allowed private merchants to travel and trade across the borders of Afghanistan. A Soviet Commercial Mission was despatched to Afghanistan in 1924, which remained there for about 3 years. An Order of the Peoples' Commissariat of Foreign Trade was issued on October 23, 1925, which provided the tax-free import to Soviet territory of Afghan raw material like cattle, consumer goods and carpets; and the unlicensed export into Afghanistan of all goods of Soviet origin, except prohibited ones and a small number of contingents.[1] Afghan authorities were aware of the fact that more imports means more exploitation. So they always tried to keep the balance of trade in Afghan side.

Though, there was no formal trade agreement between the two countries, but Soviet-Afghan trade was increasing year by year. Soviet Russia had paid on March 12, 1921, 1,20.000 roubles and in August, 1921, 500,000 roubles to Afghanistan as annual subsidy promised under the Soviet-Afghan Agreement of 1921. This helped in the tremendous boost of trade between the two countries. These trade relations were interrupted in 1926, when Germany established its mercantile firm in Kabul. But on June 27, 1927, an Order was issued by the Commissariat for Foreign and Domestic Trade of Soviet Russia regarding imports from Afghanistan.[2] This consolidated the Commercial relations between the two countries. During 1923-29, the general exchange of Soviet-Afghan trade increased from 1,383,000 roubles to 18,691,000 roubles, surpassing the pre-war figures of 1913 which were 12,245,000 roubles.

The Soviet Commissar for Foreign Trade had provided the free import into Soviet Russia from Afghanistan of agricultural produce and raw materials without a licence; and also that the export from Soviet Russia to Afghanistan of industrial

Soviet Afghan Trade 1923-29[3]

(In Roubles)[4]

Years	*Exports to Afghanistan*	*Imports from Afghanistan*	*Turnover*
1923-24	69,000	1,314,000	1,383,000
1924-25[5]	978,000	1,641,000	2,619,000
1925-26	2,495,000	3,429,000	5,924,000
1926-27	3,421,000	4,114,000	7,635,000
1927-28	6,863,000	6,492,000	13,335,000
1928-29[6]	7,006,000	11,685,000	18,691,000
	20,832,000	28,675,000	49,507,000

produce with the exception of sugar and oil products. Following products were exchanged between the two countries during the years 1924-1929 :

Soviet Imports from Afghanistan[7]

(In Tons)

	1924-25	*1925-26*	*1926-27*	*1927-28*	*1928-29*
Wool	1817	2636	4060	4052	4346
Cotton	342	260	487	618	1069
Astrakhan	—	—	—	85	30
Lambskin	—	—	—	85	120
Sheep and Goat Skins	—	—	—	264	621
Dry Fruits	82	135	—)		
Almonds and Pistachis	—	19	—))	61	32
	2241	3050	4547	5165	6218

(*In Roubles*)

Large Cattle	20,000	11,000	5,000	25,000	91,000
Small Cattle	54,000	5,84,000	4,36,000	7,77,000	3,77,000
	74,000	5,95,000	4,41,000	8,02,000	4,68,000

Soviet Exports from Afghanistan[8]

(*In Tons*)

	1924-25	*1925-26*	*1926-27*	*1927-28*	*1928-29*
Sugar	14	1596	2831	5063	4480
Cotton Cloth	16	200	302	902	902
Hemp and Jute Articles	13	54	51	18	49
Metal Articles	174	281	338	724	791
Oil Products	318	675	924	418	1856
Silicates	63	92	119	200	371
Matches	65	1	49	85	233
Rubber Articles	3	7	34	32	59
	666	2906	4648	7442	8739

Owing to the absence of trade treaty between the two countries, there were some restrictions on Soviet traders to penetrate directly into Afghanistan. So that Soviet exports to Afghanistan were carried out exclusively by the Afghan merchants. Hundreds of camels full of merchandise were arriving in Herat from Turkistan. There were Soviet stores retailing oil, cotton, skins, glass crockery and miscellaneous articles. It was on December 3, 1924, that Afghan Minister of Trade and Industry, Abdul Khadi Khan, stated in an interview with a Soviet Press representative that the main obstacle to the

the political structure, economic system and the cultural pattern in Indian society.

The various resolutions passed at the All India Congress Committee sessions have been analysed with a view to identifying the educational component of the political apparatus provided by the party to the Indian society. It gives a fair estimate of the party's thinking on educational matters and explains the steps taken by the Government formed by INC in the post independence period. In sum Indian National Congress worked as a mass party according to the quality of leadership at the helm of affairs at a particular time. Otherwise the party has been having a conservative image and has always been dominated by the bourgeoise, feudal and capitalistic elements and so has been minimally successful in radicalising Indian education and the society. But it must be credited with the huge expansion of Indian education in the post independence period.

It was Allen Octavian Hume a man of the immense fellow feeling and infinite courage who conceived the necessity of a "national union", to be an intermediary between the government and the people, over whore pitiable plight his mind was greatly perturbed."[1] It was on December 28, 1885, in the hall of the Gokul Das Tejpal Sanskrit College, Bombay, that the First National Congress met.

Some British people like Lord Dufferin thought that Indian National Congress should act like His Majesty's opposition. Hume was in favour of Congress taking aline of above party politics and should, have therefore, supported the Government. But later it is stated that Hume accepted the view of the role of opposition for the Congress.

During the first 14 years of its inception, the Indian National Congress remained a body merely submitting humble petitions and representations but in 1899, in its Lucknow session it announced that its object was to promote by constitutional means, the interests and the well-being of the people of the Indian Empire. The Congress in those days was a body of the English educated Indian aristocracy seeking opportunities for government employment and other favours.[2] The beneficiaries of the English education were mostly the upper caste Brahmins and Kayasthas. Swami Viveka Nand was highly critical of this bourgeoise mentality and favoured the awakening of the masses. Mrs. Annie Besant and Bal Ganga Dhar Tilak tried to convert Congress into a mass based organisation. "The eminent liberals of India endowed it with grace, dignity and intellectual poise."[3] From this foundation, it became possible for M.K. Gandhi to make INC a big mass appealing and mass moving power. Later Subash Chandra Bose energized the Congress with the dynamic Youth of this country. This youth power gave Congress the energy to launch a revolution.

It has been stated about Congress,

"The INC, which was originally an intellectual association to ventilate the grievances of mostly the vested interests, was thus transformed into on all embracing mass organization so accomodative as to permit the capitalist and the communist the feudalist and the socialist, the reactionary and the revolutionary, the conservative and the radical the bigot and the atheist, the casteist and the out caste, to function freely with in its fold for the one object of achieving the independence of the nation."[4]

"In the whole world there is perhaps no political party which altogether resembles it. It is a collection of almost every conceivable interest and type of personality." . . . "Like Hinduism itself, it finds room for every opinion, every class, and every eccentricity."

The Congress became the major political force through an eventful history comprising four periods, the age of humble petition and appeal, the age of constitutional liberalism, the age of uncompromising extremism and the age of non-cooperation and direct-action, before it reached the age of political power. Although it has reduced itself from a national movement to a fection ridden political party, it is still the biggest political organization strong enough to monopolize power, to the exclusion of its rivals."[5]

It is said that during Nehru period after the death of Sardar Patel, Congress Party became over confident and even did not provide the basic essentials of democracy. It developed a belief that it could not be replaced by any other political force and could retain power through cleverly managed permutations and combinations[6] Towards the end of Nehru era, it realized its decline in popularity, its losing hold over the people. It could not shed off its inherent traditionalism and it suffered from inaction which forced many of its follows to quit this party.

The Provincial Congress leaders became fairly assertive and began to oppose Nehru in the party forums. Nehru wisely concieved a plan, known as Kamraj Plan and tried to oust Chief Ministers and Cabinet Ministers opposed to him. It is said that Nehru era had started with the death of Sardar Patel and ended with the presidency of Kamraj. But the effects of Nehru's planning in organizational matters were bound to last long.

Sadasivasan has rightly observed that the election of MPs, Indira Gandhi in 1966 by outmanoeuvring the supporters of Morarji Desai, as planned by Kamraj, marked the beginning of a period of bitter fighting inside the Congeess. It was incidentally also a period of decline in democratic morals, gainful defection and flourishing political opportunism. Indeed, the struggle in the Congress was essentially between traditionalization of power and its federalization. And the victory was determined in favour of the former by military and risk taking. Never before was Congress politics so sensitive and disparate at the national level.

At the time of election of Lal Bahadur Shastri as Prime Minister, the politics of consensus had played a part but during Indira Gandhi's term, the consensus politics gave way to division.

Rajinder Puri a noted cartoonist and journalist found that the decision taking processes of Mrs. Gandhi and her public ulterances were rather childish and did great harm to the growth of a healthy democratic convention in India.[7] According to him Mrs. Indira Gandhi in fact indulged in unscrupulous and immoral political relations. That Mrs. Gandhi had in fact given a rude shock to the credibility of the political institutions of the country.

Puri was of the view that the essentially federal character of India's constitution had been blurred by two decades of rule both at the centre and in most of the states by the same political party, Congress of Indira Gandhi.[8]

A very senior Congressman and a former Chief Minister of Delhi, Chowdhary Braham Parkash, was of the view that while as Nehru was a charismatic leader, because he was loved by the general public, but Indira Gandhi was not loved by the public, she was only feared and as such she was not a charismatic leader. Chowdhary Braham Parkash felt 'that Mrs. Gandhi bade good bye to all political morality and she was responsible for rampant corruption which entered into the body politic of national life during her rule.[9]

Congress Ideology

The Indian National Congress has always been a national movement but the party lacks strict party character. These remarks were made by no less than an Indian sociologist A. Narashimha Reddy. He observed,

> "Unlike modern political parties, Congress Party has no well knit organisation on modern lines. Like its present organisation, the Congress Party in Andhra Pradesh is a mass party and lacks cadre. It has inherited all the qualities of parent body. It is predominantly rural in its nature and the back bone of the party is landed gentry. The character of the party has been changing from time to time. Before independence the Congress Party was

dominated by the educated urban elite. In terms of caste, the Brahmins predominated".[10]

After independence, however, the composition of the party had changed. In case of Andhra Pradesh the landed gentry (mostly non Brahmin upper castes) slowly began to occupy, which was a case almost everywhere the important positions of the party. Their numerical strength had become an important factor. The principal castes of landed gentry are Reddies, Kammas, Kapus, Kshatriyas and Velamas.

He wrote "with the formation of Andhra state the party character was basically altered. The principal castes of landed gentry have a complete sway over the party". He further said, with the introduction of Panchayatti Raj institutions, this particular class became powerful in the party.

This dominance of the landed gentry in Congress politics has a relevance for education. Almost all the posts of Vice-Chancellors in the states were given to the dominant caste people, whose Chief Minister was in power. It is significant to point out that the editor of the above mentioned book Shri G. Ram Reddy became Vice Chancellor of Osmania University, which was basically a Muslim University and he became Vice Chancellor of the first open university in Andhra due to caste policies. This phenomenon prevailed in all the states in India.

It is said that from 1972 to 1977 during Indira Gandhi's Prime Ministership this trend was changed. But only in name, otherwise the caste politics dominated and this had a relevance for education also.

Commenting on the party character and the party base, Mr. Rao said that Congress has no specific class character. It is not a cadre based party; it is difficult to know the character of the party. It is difficult to agree that it is the dominantly rural based party. At the national level it is dominated by the industrialists, capitalists and the petty bourgeoise. Caste and regional loyalities have always generated tension and heat in the Congress party.[11]

Dr. Shankar Dayal Sharma, President of All India Congress Committee in a letter addressed to all the Presidents of PCCS and DCCS, (Pradeshik and District Congress Committees) had written that two vitally important resolutions were passed by the AICC (All India Congress Committee) at its meeting at Gandhi Nagar Gujarat on October, 9 and 10, 1972. The second resolution had dealt with the basic issues of economic policy and the strategy to be adopted by the party and government, both at the Centre and in the states, for achieving the national objectives of self reliance and elimination of poverty He wrote,

> "Broadly speaking the party must accomplish two tasks. First, the party has to engage itself in ceaselessly educating the basic direction of our social and economic policies. An attempt is being made by some political parties in the country to confuse the people over basic issues by taking advantages of certain trends in our economy which we are trying to correct with all our force. We have to expose the underlying motives of political parties which want to obstruct our progress towards a self reliant socialist society."[12]

Dr. Sharma had in his letter emphasised the role of the party in educating the masses about the programmes taken up by the Government in the coming Fifth Five Year Plan, which was to be executed in 1974.

In the end he wrote, "The Gandhi Nagar session has provided us with a clear blue print for action. We have now to throw ourselves into the many sided and challenging tasks of helping the people to march forward under the leadership of our Prime Minister, Shrimati Indira Gandhi towards the realisation of their cherished goal of a society free from want and from injustice."[13]

In the preindependence period the Congress had been advocating socialist politics, every one naturally looked to the Congress to bring about a new order and to improve their lot. "The consolidation and the integration of the country was important to the Congress but equally important was to find a commonly acceptable means to tackle the various problems. To maintain the harmony, unity and integrity of the nation was what they told they were interested in. But in reality the survival and hegemony of the party was what they were actually working for, but without making it too obvious. The socialist policy came in handy at a time when the Congress was on the horns of this dilemma."[14]

Commenting on the nature of the Congress organisation, she observed that the INC which was a basically middle class organisation with a very strong conservative wing, no doubt must have found it extremely difficult to keep the balance between the demands of the vested interests and the poverty struck masses.

"Although the Congress Commitment to socialism was welcomed throughout the country, it created a split among the Gandhians. The most orthodox warned that the Congress commitment was a radical departure which might cause greater defections."[15]

Concluding the remarks, it said, "In other words though progressive economic policies were accepted, attempts to fix ceilings on land holdings and the distribution of excess land with little compensation produced a number of controversies."[16]

The Socialistic Pattern of Society

The 60th session of the Indian National Congress was held at Avadi in 1955 . . . It was here for the first time that the party's avowed objective of a cooperative commonwealth was extended to include "planning with a view to establishing a socialistic pattern of society."[17]

Tribune in an editorial captioned as "The Congress Conundrum' had written that Rajiv Gandhi had expressed his determination to tone up the party machinery and loosen the hold of power brokers and influence peddlars on the Congress (I).

This was an year old question and had been heard many a times before. It concluded that two years after the death of Indira Gandhi the state of the Congress (I) remained as confused and disorganised as it was in the past decade.[18]

G.M. Telang in an article in Indian Express wrote that revolt in Congress (I) was not possible, because all those who criticised the leadership of Rajiv Gandhi, were those who had been deprived of power. Some of them like Pranab Mukherji the former Finance Minister in the Union Cabinet, Gundu Rao a former Chief Minister of Karnataka, P.C. Sethi former Home Minister of India criticised the leadership on personal ground. However on being expelled they formed Indira Congress on the plea that policies of Mrs. Indira Gandhi were being flouted. They accused Rajiv Gandhi against his style of functioning, against the scheming by his sycophants, against the domination of the Doon mafia, a self serving coterie etc. Elitism had become yet another fashionable target of caustic comments on the leadership.[19]

Tribune in a similar way observed that destabilising state governments was part and parcel of the Congress political culture in the past decade and a half. It also advised the Congressmen all over the country that it was time to give up the idea that state governments existed at their pleasure and convenience.[20]

The Indian Express called it a fragmented party in the recent past when it said that the Congress (I) in its present incarnation was a party plagued by groupism. Some of its members had never been afraid to acknowledge that it was an agglomeration of diverse and separate groupings in which parochial or vested interests some times got the better of overall party interests. "But things seem to be getting out of hand of late and as the months go by, there seems to be less and less unity in the party's diversity."[21] It concluded by saying that less than a year ago, at the Congress centenary in Bombay the Prime Minister, Mr. Rajiv Gandhi, promised action against power brokers and vested interests in his party. That he must have kept his word.

Commenting on the state of the party, Tribune observed that Congress continued to present the image of a political band wagon—large enough to invite assorted politicians to jump on rather than a mass based party. Politiking and intrigue go on all the time. It observed, "Dissidence has been a part of Congress culture, and it was accentuated after Mrs. Indira Gandhi ushered in the era of imposed Chief Ministers. The insignificant rebellion against some of the Congress (I) Chief Ministers indicates nothing more than the fact that the ruling party more or less retains the characteristics it prominently displayed under Indira Gandhi. Inner party democracy is still a distant dream. Be it U.P., Orissa or Maharashtra the players who call the political tune are those who (claim to) represent the charmed circle of favourites of the Prime Minister. When in December 1985, Mr. Rajiv Gandhi gave powerful expression to his views on the image and functioning of the Congress organisation, it was presumed that he would soon launch a thorough overhauling of the party, clean it of malcontents and restore inner party democracy. The achievement since then has been that one set of power brokers has replaced another."[22]

Congress on Education

The Indian National Congress in its Third session at Madras in 1887 had passed a resolution to move the government to elaborate a system of technical education, suitable to the condition of the country, to encourage indigenous manufacturers by a more strict observance of the orders, already existing, in regard to utilising such manufactures for state purposes and to employ more extensively there at that time the skill and talents of the people of the country.[23]

In the Fourth Congress held at Allahabad in 1888 the INC passed a resolution on Education General and Technical. The Congress was of the opinion that it was the first duty of the British Government in India to foster and encourage education general as well as technical in all its branches. The Government was urged to increase expenditure on education to keep the control in its hands.[24]

In its Seventh session held in Nagpur in 1891, the INC passed a resolution urging upon the government to provide more money for education and it also demanded the setting up of a mixed commission to enquire into the then industrial condition of the country. The emphasis of course was on technical education.[25]

The resolution on education in Eighth Congress held in 1892 in Allahabad was a repetition of the previous one.[26]

The Twelfth Congress was held in Calcutta in 1896. recorded its protest over the exclusion of Indians from the education and higher services.[27] It also resolved for opening of technical schools and for fostering local and individual manufacturers.[28] This session for the first time resolved for bringing reform in Indian universities. It demanded for the amendment of the Acts of incorporation of universities of Calcutta, Madras and Bombay for making teaching as one of their functions.[29]

In its Fourteenth session held in Madras in 1898, the Congress passed a resolution for the development of technical education including the development of local craftsmen.[30]

In its Sixteenth session held in Lahore in 1900, the Congress made a routine resolution for the development of technical education, with almost the old words repeated out and appreciation for Tata for his contribution in research work.[31] It also resolved for the appointment of a committee for the improvement of education.[32]

In its session in 1901 held in Calcutta the INC expressed satisfaction over the attention the then Viceroy was giving to educational matters and demanded greater representation on the Education Commission which was to be constituted by the Viceroy.[33]

In the eighteenth session held in Ahmedabad, the Congress for the first time made elaborate resolutions criticising the recommendations of the Commission especially the officialization of universities, senate and the syndicate and the licensing of secondary education by the making private education dependent upon recognition by the education department.[34] It was quite a comprehensive resolution as compared to the previous ones

The Nineteenth session held in 1903 in Madras, passed a long resolution on the Universities Bill and demanded more autonomy for the universities.[35]

In its Twentieth session held in Bombay in 1904, the Congress passed resolutions for the provision of more funds for primary education and for working in the direction of making it free and compulsory. It was demanded that training in manual work and scientific agriculture should be started.[36] In this way it was a clear development in regard to the Congress policy on education. It was the first land mark.

In the Twenty-First session held in 1905 in Benares, the resolutions were a repetition only of the previous year. It demanded the opening of a technical school in some central place.[37]

The Twenty-Second Congress session held in Calcutta in 1906 repeated its protest against the policy of the Government in respect of high and secondary education, as being one of officialising the governing bodies of the universities and restricting the spread of education.[38] It read,

> "That in the opinion of this Congress the time has arrived for the people all over the country earnestly to take up the question of national education, for both boys and girls and organise a system of education—literary, scientific and technical suited to the requirements of the country on National Lines under National Control."[39]

It will thus be seen that for the first time since its inception in 1885 the Indian National Congress had moved the resolution for an education on national lines and under national control.

In the Twenty-Third Congress session held in Madras in 1908 it had resolved that the Congress was of the opinion that the government should have made primary education free and gradually compulsory, should have assigned larger sums of money to secondary and higher education. The government was urged to make adequate provision for imparting industrial and technical education in the different provinces, having regard to local requirements and to give effective voice to the leaders of Indian public opinion in shaping the policy and system of education in this country.[40]

It wrote, "In the opinion of this Congress the time has arrived for people all over the country to take up earnestly the question of supplementing existing institutions and the efforts of the government by organising for themselves an independent system of literary, scientific, technical and industrial education, suited to the conditions of the different provinces in the country."[41]

In Twenty-Fourth Congress held in Lahore in 1909 the previous resolutions on education were repeated.[42]

In the Twenty-Fifth session in 1910 held in Allahabad, it took up resolutions separately on elementary education, Secondary and Higher Industrial and Technical education and on National Control on elementary education it said, that in the opinion of this Congress the time has arrived when a substantial beginning should be made in the matter of Elementary Education—free and compulsory—throughout the country."[43]

"That this Congress is of the opinion that the Government should take early steps

(a) to assign larger sums of money to secondary and higher education (special encouragement being given where necessary to educate all backward classes)

(b) to make adequate provision for imparting industrial and technical education in the different Provinces, having regard to local requirements; and

(c) to give effective voice to the leaders of Indian public opinion in shaping the policy and system of Education in this country."

That in the opinion of this Congress the time has arrived for people all over the country, to take up earnestly the question of supplementing existing institutions and the efforts of the government by organising for themselves and independent system of Literary, Scientific, Technical and Industrial Education, suited to the conditions of the different provinces in the country."[44]

In the Twenty-Sixth Congress held in Calcutta in 1911, the Congress accorded wholehearted support to the principles of the Hon. Mr. Gokhale's Elementary Education Bill.[45]

The rest of the recommendations were repetitions of the previous resolutions in regard to Higher and Technical Education for peoples participation in the education of the Indian people.

In the Twenty-Seventh Congress session in 1912 in Bankipore it expressed its satisfaction and thoughtfulness that the government had announced a more active educational policy, it regretted the defeat of the Hon. Mr. Gokhale's Elementary Education Bill and affirmed its conviction that the introduction of a measure of free and compulsory education was essential to secure a rapid extension of Elementary Education.[46]

In its Twenty-Eighth session held in 1913 in Karachi, the Congress while thanking the Government of India for its donations of larger grants towards the extension of Primary Education in India expressed the strong opinion that a beginning was then to be made for introducing free and compulsory education in some selected areas.

The Congress passed the following resolutions:

(a) That this Congress, while approving of the proposals

by government for introducing teaching and residential universities is strongly of opinion that that system should supplement and not replace the existing system of university education, as otherwise the progress of Higher Education among the poorer classes will be seriously retarded.

(b) That this Congress reciterates its prayer to government to make adequate provision for imparing Industrial and Technical Education in the different provinces, having regard to local requirements.

(c) That this Congress records its strong protest against the action of the Government of India vetoing the selection by the Calcutta University of Messers, Rasul, Suhravardi and Jayaswal, as lecturers, on the grounds of their connection with politics; as the ban of politics is so general as to lend itself to arbitrary exclusion of the best scholarship from the lecturers' chair, so deterimental to the interests of education in the country. In this way Congress protested against the political considerations of the Government of India in vetoing the selection of lecturers.[47]

It is significant to note that the Congress in its Twenty-Ninth session held in Madras in 1914, desired to convey to His Majesty the King Emperor and the People of England, its profound devotion to the Throne, its unswerving allegiance to the British connection, and its firm resolve to stand by the Empire, at all hazards and at all costs.[48]

These were the First World War times and the Congress had extended its unfailing loyalties to the British crown.

The Twentieth Congress was held in 1915 in Bombay. The Congress expressed its protest against the discriminations being shown against Indian students in the Universities of England.[49]

The Twenty-First Congress session was held in 1916 in Lucknow. It resolved as under :

The Patna University Bill

> This Congress places on record its emphatic protest against the highly retrograde character of the Patna University Bill, and strongly urges that it should be so amended as to make it a thoroughly liberal and progressive measure.

This Congress passed other important resolutions on education, which demanded more and more representation of Indian in educational services and on university senates. It demanded that in matters of grant in aid to students discrimination against Indian students in favour of British students should be dispensed with. It demanded the introduction of compulsory and free elementary education. It urged for starting more and more industrial and commercial schools. It exhorted voluntary organizations to start their schools. It also resolved against compulsory religious education in Govt. aided schools.[50]

Mrs. Besant in her presidential address in Calcutta in 1917 emphasised on Home Rule idea and it gained momentum. Linked with this was the idea of linguistic provinces. The importance of language as the basis of the provincial demarcation was accepted by the Congress this year.[51] Linguistic provinces were seen as an essential condition prerequisite to real provincial autonomy.[52]

The 1918 session of All India Congress Committee was held in Bombay in which Montague Chelmsford proposals were discussed.

The Twenty-Third session of the Congress was held in Delhi on 26th December 1918. Pandit Madan Mohan Malviya was the president.

The Amritsar Congress of 1919 was a triumph for national self respect.[53]

In 1921, the 36th session was held in Ahmedabad. This session endorsed the resolution of attainment of Swaraj, the complete freedom through civil disobedience, through individual non-cooperation and civil non-cooperation. Non-cooperation and non-violence, later became the cult of the freedom struggle. This session appointed Mahatma Gandhi as the sole executive authority of the Congress and invested him with the full powers of the All India Congress Committee.[54] A new phase in the life of Congress started.

The 37th session was held in Gaya in 1922. The session passed a resolution on education and declared "that the boycott must be maintained, and further resolved that every province should be called upon to put the existing national institutions on a sound financial basis and to improve their efficiency in every possible way."[55] Education thus became a political weapon in the hands of Congress.

The Thirty-Eighth session was held in 1923 at CACI Nada. No worthwhile resolution on education was passed in this session.

The Thirty-Ninth session of the Indian National Congress assembled in Belgaum on 26th December 1924. It was unique for Congress unity. The presidential address of Mahatma Gandhi on national schools is an important development.

The Fortieth session of INC was held in Kanpur in 1925. From education point of view it had only resolved that the proceedings of INC sessions should be written in Hindustani.

The Forty-First session of INC was held in Gauhati in 1926. Nothing specifically was resolved about education in this session.

The Forty-Second session was held in 1927 in Madras. This session passed a resolution for complete Indian independence.

Federated Soviet Republic on Afghan territory and of seven consulates of Afghanistan on Russian territory, of which five shall be within the boundaries of Russian Central Asia.

Note : In addition to the above, the opening of further consulates and consular points in Russia and Afghanistan shall be arranged in each particular case by special agreement between the High Contracting Parties.

5. Russian Consulates shall be established at Herat, Meimen Mazar-i-Sharif, Kandahar and Ghazni. Afghan Consulates shall be established as follows :—

A Consulate-General at Tashkent and Consulates at Petrograd, Kazan, Samarkand, Merv and Krasnovodsh.

Note : The manner and time of the actual opening of the Russian Consulates in Afghanistan and of the Afghan Consulates in Russia shall be defined by special agreement between the two contracting parties.

6. Russia agrees to the free and untaxed transit through her territory of all kinds of goods purchased by Afghanistan either in Russia herself, through State Organisation, or from abroad.

7. The High Contracting Parties recognize and accept the freedom of Eastern Nations on the basis of independence and in accordance with the general wish of each nation.

8. In confirmation of clause 7 of the present Treaty, the High Contracting Parties accept the actual independence and freedom of Bukhara and Khiva, whatever may be the form of their government, in accordance with the wishes of their people.

9. In fulfilment and in accordance with the promise of the Russian Socialist Federated Soviet Republic, expressed by Lenin as its head, to the Minister Plenipotentiary of the sovereign state of Afghanistan, Russia agrees to hand over to Afghanistan the frontier districts which belonged to the latter in the last century,observing the principles of justice and self-determination of the populaion inhabiting the same. The manner in which such self-determination and will of the majority of the regular local population shall be expressed, shall be settled by a special treaty between the two states intermediary of plenipotentiaries of both parties.

10 In order to strengthen friendly relations between the High Contracting Parties, the Government of the Russian Socialist Federated Soviet Republic agrees to give to Afghanistan financial and other assistance.

I1 The present Treaty is drown up in the Russian and Persian languages; both texts are accounted authentic.

12. The present Treaty shall come into force upon its ratification by the Governments of the High Contracting Parties. The exchange of ratification shall take place at Kabul, in witness whereof the plenipotentiaries of both parties have signed the present Treaty and set their seals thereto.

Drawn up in Moscow on the 28th day of February, 1921.

Supplemental Clause

In amplification of clause 10 of the present Treaty, the Government of the Russian Socialist Federated Soviet Republic gives the following assistance to the sovereign state of Afghanistan :

1. A yearly free subsidy to the extent of one million gold or silver roubles in coins or bullion.

2. Construction of the Kushk-Herat Kandahar-Kabul telegraph line.

3. In addition to this, the Government of the Russian Socialist Federated Soviet Republic expresses its readiness to place at the disposal of the Afghan Government technical and other specialists.

The Government of the Russian Socialist Federated Soviet Republic shall afford this assistance to the Government of Sovereign State of Afghanistan which two months after the coming into force of the present Treaty.

The present supplementary clause shall have the same legal validity as the other clauses of the present Treaty.

Moscow, this 28th day of February, 1921.

II—PROTOCOL REGARDING THE QUESTION OF UTRA-TAGAI ISLAND

(Kabul: August 15, 1926)

The Protocol was drawn up by a joint Afghan-Soviet Commission composed of :

Delegation of Afghan Government :

President — Aqai Mirza Muhammad Khan

Members — Ghulam Yahya Khan
Ali Akbar Khan.

Delegation of the USSR

Offg.
President — Monsiewe B.P. Postnikoff

Member — Colonel A.M. Rix.

The Protocol contains the following clauses :

1. The Joint Afghan-Soviet Commission recognized it useless to continue to discuss by either of the parties the question regarding the ownership of the Island of Utra-Tagai on legal and historical grounds.

2. On behalf of its Government, the Commission of the USSR, having regard to the unchangeable friendly relations between the USSR and the exalted Government of Afghanistan and with the object of strengthening these relations, recognises the importance of the predominating economic advantage of the Island of Utra-Tagai to the Exalted Government of Afghanistan. The Commission of the USSR, therefore, agrees to the reception of the Island into the complete ownership of the Exalted Government of Afghanistan.

3. The two Commissions, on behalf of their respective Governments, agree that a period of six months should be granted to the people of the Island for the final

selection by them, in accordance with their own desire, of a place of residence in the territory of either of the parties, and in that case no interference will be made with the emigration of those people with the whole of their belongings who may desire to do so. This period of six months is to be reckoned from the date of signing of the protocol.

4. Both the Commissions agree that with a view to giving this Protocol a final legal form, the agreement of the two Governments to the text of this Protocol should be confirmed by exchange of notes between His Excellency, the Minister of Foreign Affairs, on behalf of the Exalted Government of Afghanistan; and His Excellency, the Minister plenipotentiary, on behalf of the USSR.

5. This Protocol had been drawn up in two copies in the Persian and Russian languages, both texts having equal force.

Kabul, this 15th day of August, 1926.

III—SOVIET AFGHAN TREATY OF RECIPROCAL NEUTRALITY AND NON-AGGRESSION

(With Protocol)
(Paghman: August 31, 1926)

Treaty of reciprocal neutrality and non-aggression between the exalted Government of Afghanistan and the Government of the Union Soviet Socialist Republics with the object of confirming the friendly relations and of strengthening the friendly neighbourly connection which happily, based on the Treaty signed in Moscow on the 28th February, 1921, subsist between the Exalted Governments of Afghanistan and the Union of Soviet Socialist Republics. The said Treaty preserves its force in all its parts irrespective of continuance or cancellation of the present Treaty.

The plenipotentiaries of the exalted parties, His Excellency the Minister of Foreign Affairs of the exalted Government of Afghanistan, Aqai Mahmud Beg Khan Tarzi, and His Excellency the Minister plenipotentiary of the Union of Soviet Socialist Republics in Afghanistan, Aqai Leonid Stark, after exchanging their lawful credentials, which were found correct, on the 31st August, 1926, at Paghman, framed and signed these articles, the object of which is to strengthen the friendly relations between the two governments and to ensure permanent peace.

Article 1

In case of war or military action between one of the contracting parties and one or more third powers, the other contracting party undertakes to observe neutrality towards the first party.

Article 2

Each of the contracting parties undertakes to abstain from all kinds of aggression against the other, and will not even within the territory under its own occupation takes any such steps as may cause political or military injury to the other contracting Government. In particular each of the contracting parties undertakes that it will not join with another state or states in any political or military alliance or union directed against the other contracting party, and similarly it will not join in any boycot or financial and cconomic blockade directed against the other. In addition to this, should the policy of third party state or states be hostile in its action to either of the contracting parties, the other contracting party undertakes not only to abstain from assisting such hostile policy but also to prevent the said policy and inimical actions and steps within its own territory.

Article 3

The high contracting parties, each reciprocally recognizing the sovereignty and integrity of the other, undertakes to abstain from all kinds of armed and unarmed interference in the internal affairs of the other contracting party and also not to join or assist any other state or states, which may take steps against, or interfere with, the other contracting state.

The contracting parties will not permit any groups or individuals in their own territories to establish or to prosecute activities detrimental to the other contracting party; or to take steps for the subversion of the established government of the other against the integrity of the territory of the other contracting party; or to mobilise or collect armed forces against the other contracting party; and will prevent them from taking action. Similarly the parties will not countenance the transit through their territories of any armed forces, arms, firearms, ammunitions, or the supply of any kind of war materials intended (for use) against the other contracting party, and likewise will (take active steps to) prevent the same from passing through its territory.

Article 4

The contracting parties agree within four months to enter into discussions to determine principles for the solution of differences which may arise between them, and which cannot be settled through the ordinary diplomatic channels.

Article 5

Each of the contracting parties, outside the limits of undertakings, the conditions of which are defined in this Treaty, has freedom of action in taking steps to form any kind of relations and any kind of agreement with other states.

Article 6

From the date of ratification, which should not be more than three months after it has been signed, this Treaty will have the force of law and will remain in force for three years. After the expiration of the said period it will be understood that the Treaty continues for a year more automatically unless either of the contracting parties has notified to the other party, six months before the expiration of the period, its desire to terminate the enforcement of this Treaty.

Article 7

Two copies of this treaty have been written, in Persian and in Russian, and both texts will have equal forces.

Done at Paghman on the 31st August, 1926, corresponding to the Sumbala, 1305.

Mahmud Beg Tarzi,
Foreign Minister

L.H. Stark,
Minister Plenipotentiary
of the Union of Soviet
Socialist Republics.

Protocol : Of the Treaty of reciprocal neutrality and non-aggression contracted between the Exalted Governments of Afghanistan and the Union of Soviet Socialist Republics—Paghman, 1305.

The following signatories, who were correctly empowered to sign the Treaty of reciprocal neutrality and non-aggression between the Government of the Union of Soviet Socialist Republics and the Exalted Government of Afghanistan, by permission of their respective Governments, have exchanged the following statement on the occasion of signing the said Treaty.

His Excellency Aqai Leonid Stark, Minister Plenipotentiary in Afghanistan of the Union of Soviet Socialist Republics, states that he has received permission from the Government of the Union of Soviet Socialist Republics to certify in the name of his Government that, on the occasion of signing the above Treaty, the Government of the Union of Soviet Socialist Republics, having been faithful to the principles of the Treaty of the 28th February, 1921, has no agreement with any state or states contrary to the Treaty contracted on the 31st August, 1926, regarding reciprocal neutrality and non-aggression. Similarly, he states on behalf of his Government that the Government of the Union of Soviet Socialist Republics certifies that, during the whole of the period for which this Treaty of reciprocal neutrality and non-aggression remains in force, the said Government will not enter into such treaties or conventions as may be contrary to this Treaty of reciprocal neutrality and non-aggression. The Union of Soviet Socialist Republics trusts that the friendly relations between the Governments of the Union of Soviet Socialist Republics and Afghanistan, based on the Treaty contracted in Moscow on the 28th February, 1921, and on the Treaty contracted at Paghman on the 31st August, 1926, will invariably increase and will be based on the lofty ideal of general peace.

His Excellency Aqai Mahmud Beg Khan Tarzi, Minister of Foreign Affairs of the Exalted Government of Afghanistan, states that he has received permission from the Afghan Government to certify in the name of his Government that, on the occasion of signing the above Treaty, the Afghan Government, having been faithful to the principles of the Treaty of the 28th February, 1921, has no agreement with any state or states contrary to the Treaty contracted on the 31st August, 1926, regarding reciprocal neutrality and non-aggression. Similarly, he states on behalf of his Government that the Afghan Government certifies that, during the whole of the period for which this Treaty or reciprocal neutrality and non-aggression remains in force, the said Government will not enter into such treaties or conventions as may be contrary to this Treaty of reciprocal neutrality and non-aggression. The Afghan Government trusts that friendly relations between the Governments of Afghanistan and the Union of Soviet Socialist Republics, based on the Treaty contracted in Moscow on the 28th February, 1921, and on the Treaty contracted at Paghman on 31st August, 1926, will invariably increase and will be based on the lofty ideal of general peace.

In confirmation of the above the following signatures have framed this Protocol.

Done at Paghman on the 31st August, 1926, in two copies, in Russian and in Persian, both texts having equal force. 31st August, 1926, corresponding to the 8th Sumbala, 1305.

Mahmud Beg Tarzi,
Foreign Minister of
Afghanistan.

L.H. Stark,
Minister Plenipotentiary
of the Union of Soviet
Socialist Republics.

VI—AGREEMENT BETWEEN THE GOVERNMENT OF USSR AND THE EXALTED GOVERNMENT OF AFGHANISTAN REGARDING KABUL-TASHKENT AIR ROUTE

(Kabul: November 28, 1927)

On the 28th November 1927, at Kabul the Government of the USSR, through M. Leonid Nikolaievitch Stark, Minister Plenipotentiary of the USSR in Afghanistan, of the one part, and the Afghan Government, through M. Ghulam Sadiq Khan, Officiating Foreign Minister of the Afghan Government, of the other part, contracting the following Agreement for the purpose of establishing relations for the regulation of postal and passenger aerial traffic between Kabul and Tashkent :

1. From the machines at their disposal, the Afghan and the USSR Governments will each provide ten aeroplanes and necessary personnel for employment on the Kabul-Tashkent air route. Movements of aeroplanes from Tashkent to Kabul shall be regulated by a time table, and flights shall be made twice in each month according to time table, but, whenever necessary machines will be despatched in addition to the above.

2. The Afghan Government will construct and provide in their territory landing-grounds, aerodromes, equipment and material necessary for the maintenance of the said air route, and undertakes to maintain the same in proper condition.

3. The Government of the USSR will construct and provide in their territory landing-grounds, aerodromes, equipment and material necessary and undertakes to maintain the same in proper condition.

4. The Government of the USSR agrees to supply to the headquarters of the Afghan Air Force spare petrol, fuel and lubricating oil for the Kabul-Tashkent air route at

the prices at which these are obtainable on the air routes of the USSR.

5. Personal supplied for the said air route by USSR will be paid by the Government of the USSR. In the same manner personnel supplied by the Afghan Government will be paid by the Government of Afghanistan. The Government of Afghanistan and the Government of the USSR will introduce to each other the names of their respective pilots and machines serving on this air route.

6. Both parties undertake to maintain stores of fuel lubricating oil, necessary material and spares sufficient for the equipment of the aeroplanes of both employed on the said air route, and each party agrees to fix beforehand, in accordance with the rates prevailing in their own territory, the price of the necessary material to be supplied to the other party.

7. The Legation of the USSR in Kabul and the Afghan Foreign Office will in the month of January make adjustments of accounts and payments due by one party to the other for the proceeding year in respect of fuel, lubricating oil, other material and spares taken or used by the aeroplanes of one party in the territory of the other, and also of all other expenditure incurred in connection with the said air route.

8. If an aeroplane belonging to one party meets with an accident in the territory of the other party, the latter will repair the aeroplane at the expense of the party to which the aeroplane belongs. The party, in the territory of which the accident has taken place, will take the machine to its workshops. If the machine is repairable and the owner agrees to pay for the repairs, the said machine will be repaired and will be taken by air to the country to which it belongs. If, however, repairs are not practicable, the party in the territory of which the accident has taken place will take and deliver the machine at

the border of the territory of the party to which the machine belongs.

9. In their respective territories each party undertakes to render full assistance to the personnel of the air service of the other party, and this more especially in case of forced landings.

10. Both parties undertake to make arrangements for customs control in both directions.

11. The tariff of fares for passengers and posts between Kabul, Termez and Tashkent will, in accordance with Article 14, be fixed by a special Agreement, which Agreement will come into operation not later than the Ist January, 1928.

12. Expenditure incurred by either party, for maintaining and looking after the air route and for providing and keeping the ground, equipment and material, and for fuel, lubricating oil, spares repairs, looking after the machine and entertainment of air personnel, will be borne by that party.

In the same way, income obtained from the use of the aeroplanes supplied by either party will be utilized according to the orders of the party concerned.

13. Passenger and postal charges will be collected in the following manner :

At Tashkent and Termez by the Central Asia Department (Dubrolet) in case of flights from Tashkent and Termez to Kabul in a USSR machine and at Tashkent by the Afghan Consul-General in case of flights in an Afghan machine.

At Kabul through the Legation of the USSR and the Headquarters, Afghan Air Force, in case of flights from Kabul to Termez rnd Tashkent.

14. Details necessary to operation of the Agreement the preparation and alteration of time-tables, matters connected with the completion of the air route and the location of landing-grounds and the preparation of fare-tables will be undertaken direct between the Dubrolet of the USSR and the Headquarters of the Afghan Air Force.

15. This Agreement will have legal force from the date on which it is signed, and flights will commence not later than the Ist January, 1928.

16. This Agreement will be acted upon till the Ist January, 1929.

17. This Agreement has been drawn up in two copies, in Russian and Persian, both having equal force.

V—AGREEMENT BETWEEN THE AERIAL DEPARTMENT OF THE U.S.S.R. AND THE AFGHAN AIR FORCE REGARDING THE KABUL-TASHKENT AIR ROUTE

(Kabul: March 7, 1928)

In order to carry out Article 14 of the Agreement of the Tashkent-Kabul Air Line, concluded between the Afghan Government and the Government of the USSR, the following agreement was concluded at Kabul on the 7th March, 1928, between the Headquarters of the Afghan Air Force and the Aerial Department of the USSR which will hereafter be called "Dubrolet" with regard to Tashkent-Kabul Air Line, through the following persons :

On behalf of the Headquarters of the Afghan Air Force, Mr. Muhammad Ihsan Khan;

On behalf of the Dubrolet of the U.S.S.R., Mr. Charneyakoff.

Article 1

In order to carry out the Agreement of November 28th, 1927, regarding the Kabul-Tashkent Air Line, the Headquarters of the Afghan Air Force appoint its representative in the Afghan Consulate General at Tashkent and the Dubrolet of the USSR appoint its agent in the USSR Legation at Kabul. The said Agents will be responsible for dealing with all matters concerning the Kabul-Tashkent Air Line.

Article 2

In completion of Article 1 of the Agreement of November 28th, 1927, the Contracting Parties appoint for the services of the Kabul-Tashkent Air Line only those persons who are subjects of the two governments. In fact those persons who were subjects of another government and subsequently adopted Afghan nationality cannot be regarded Afghan subjects.

Article 3

The Headquarters of the Afghan Air Force agrees to construct and prepare not later Ist August, 1928, landing grounds, each of which will not be less than 500×500 metres, marked with circles and angles for recognition, at the following places :

1. Haibak.
2. Any convenient place between Haibak and Khanjan.
3. Any convenient place at Khanjan.
4. Any convenient place between Khanjan and Charikar.

The ground Nos. 2 and 4 should, if possible, be prepared in a central position between the place mentioned

Article 4

The landing ground at Haibak should be equipped with accessories and material mentioned in list 1, appended to this Agreement (not published).

Article 5

The Dubrolet of the USSR makes over duly prepared and organized landing grounds within the territory of the USSR, for the Air Line of Termez, Somsonova, Samarkand and Tashkent.

Article 6

In completion of Article 4 of the Agreement of November 28th, 1927, the Headquarters of the Afghan Air Force and the Dubrolet of the USSR, agree to keep ready stocks of petrol for fuel and lubricating oil, together with accessories within their respective territories, for each other's aircraft and will issue them to each other according to the prices settled by the parties.

Article 7

If the Headquarters of the Afghan Air Force desires, the Dubrolet of the USSR will supply accessories, fuel and lubricating oil for the Kabul-Tashkent Air Line at a reasonable price.

Article 8

In pursuance of Article 5 of the Agreement of November 28th, 1927, the following aviators have been appointed by the Headquarters of the Afghan Air Force :

1. Mr. Kamenski William Fred Renchwich
2. Mechanic—Mr. Alexander Aiwinwich

Othe men for the line, to the number required, will be appointed later.

The following aviators have been appointed by the Dubrolet of the USSR :

Pilots —	Mr. Soranish Ado Ardaunwich Mr. Sinoff Michael Sawinwich Mr. Leohinko Victor Gregorywich Mr. Barnoff Nikoloi Actanowich
Mechanics —	Sovinski Watslaff Aiwanwich Nozonikoff Alexanderwich Leskoff Yafoof Wasiwich Penketkin Evin Romanwich
Reserve Pilots —	Mr. Sivoff Mavoriky Mr. Eivenoff Lahtar
Reserve Mechanics —	Moralaskin Zana Makhsaky

Article 9

The Headquarters of the Afghan Air Force agrees to

prepare and provide hostels at Mazar and Kabul for the comfort of the airmen of the Dubrolet of the USSR attached to the Kabul-Tashkent Air Line.

Article 10

It is necessary that the aviators employed on the Kabul-Tashkent Air Line should hold necessary passports with free visas, valid for the period of one year, for entering and leaving the territories of the parties without any limit of flights.

Article 11

The profits derived from the reciprocal use of the Tashkent-Kabul Air Line will be shared by the Headquarters of the Afghan Air Force and the Dubrolet of the USSR, through the Afghan Foreign Office and the USSR Legation in Afghanistan.

Article 12

In completion of Article 7 of the Agreement of November 28th, 1927, the contracting parties agree, in order to facilitate mutual accounts in respect of accessories, fuel and lubricating oil, to settle their accounts quarterly, i.e. on the Ist April, Ist June, Ist October and Ist January.

Article 13

In completion of Article 8 of the Agreement of November 28th, 1927, the Headquarters of the Afghan Air Force agrees that if an aeroplane belonging to the Dubrolet of the USSR is damaged within Afghan territory, and the Dubrolet does not approve the repair of the damaged machine in the Afghan workshops, the said Headquarters will send, at its own cost, the aeroplane to the border of the USSR Government. The Dubrolet on its side agrees that if an Afghan aeroplane is damaged within the territory of the USSR and if the Headquarters of the Afghan Force does not approve the repair of the aeroplane in the workshop of the Dubrolet of the USSR at Tashkent, the said Dubrolet will send at its own expense the damaged aeroplane to the border of the Afghan Government. The despatch of aeroplanes on both sides will be effected with the least possible delay.

Article 14

The fare for passengers is fixed as follows :

Single fare between Kabul and Tashkent	£ 27 and 10 Shillings English or 260 gold Roubles.
Single fare between Kabul and Termez	£ 16 and 10 Shillings English or 166 gold Roubles.
Single fare between Kabul and Mazar	£ 14 English or 130 gold Roubles.
Single fare between Mazar and Tashkent	£ 13 and 15 Shillings English or 135 gold Roubles.
Single fare between Mazar and Termez	£ 2 and 10 Shillings English or 26 gold Roubles.

Article 15

The fares for transport of passengers, mail and goods in a Soviet aeroplane at the time of flight from Kabul, will be collected at Kabul by the Agent to the Dubrolet in the USSR Legation in Afghanistan. Similarly, fares for transport of passengers, mail and goods in Afghan aeroplane at the time of flight from Tashkent will be collected by the Agent of the Headquarters of the Afghan Air Force in the Afghan Consulate General at Tashkent.

Article 16

Each passenger is entitled to take with him luggage up to 8 kilograms free. Any luggage in excess of 8 kilograms will be charged as follows :

One Kilogram of Luggage

Between Tashkent and Kabul	8 Shillings or $3\frac{1}{2}$ gold Roubles

Between Termez and Kabul	5 Shillings or 2 gold Roubles
Between Termez and Mazar	1 Shilling or 50 Copecks
Between Mazar and Kabul	3 Shillings or 9 pence or 1½ gold Roubles

One Kilogram of Diplomatic Mail

Between Tashkent and Kabul	12 Shillings or 5 gold Roubles and 70 Copecks.
Between Termez and Kabul	5 Shillings or 2 gold Roubles

Article 17

The following landing-grounds have been fixed:

A. Within Afghan Territory :
   1. Kabul
   2. Mazar (according to requirements)

B. Within the territory of the USSR
   1. Tashkent
   2. Termez

Article 18

The time-table of flights of aeroplanes has been arranged as follows :

Departure of Soviet aeroplane from Tashkent	28th of each month
Departure of Afghan aeroplane from Tashkent	18th of each month
Arrival of Soviet aeroplane at Termez	28th of each month
Arrival of Afghan aeroplane at Termez	18th of each month

Departure from Termez and arrival at Kabul :

of Soviet aeroplane	29th of each month
of Afghan aeroplane	19th of each month

Departure from Kabul :

of Afghan aeroplane	15th of each month
of Soviet aeroplane	1st of each month

Arrival at Termez and Tashkent :

of Afghan aeroplane	15th of each month
of Soviet aeroplane	1st of each month

If, on any of the days fixed in the time-table, the weather conditions should be unfavourable, the aeroplanes will start on the nearest subsequent day when the conditions appear more favourable. Flights, apart from those in the table, can be carried out provided arrangements may be made by the party concerned. If on the day of departure of an aeroplane there are no passengers, the aeroplane will not postpone its flight but will leave with the mail.

Article 19

The contracting parties agree to undertake the responsibility of taking all steps for the protection of aeroplanes during their stay in their respective territories, but if an aeroplane gets damaged by some extraordinary disaster, or by an act of God, the contracting parties will not be held responsible for the same. However, if damage to an aeroplane takes place owing to neglect of the guard over it, an enquiry will be held by a Commission of the parties concerned and compensation up to the damage suffered, will be paid by the party concerned. Similarly, both parties agree to give help and technical assistance as far as possible to each other's aeroplanes during their stay in their respective territories.

Article 20

Problems which arise in the course of the running on the line will be decided and settled directly by discussions held at Tashkent between the Agent of the Headquarters of the Afghan Air Force and the Dubrolet of the USSR, and at Kabul between the Agent of the Dubrolet of the USSR, and the Headquarters of the Afghan Air Force.

Article 21

The control of customs with regard to non-diplomatic persons will be effected according to the rules and regulations of the parties.

Article 22

Examination of passports is necessary before an aeroplane starts.

Article 23

If an aeroplane postpones its flight and does not start on the due date, telegraphic information must be given by one side to the other. If an aeroplane starts on the appointed day and does not reach its destination, the side concerned will give telegraphic information; and, if an aeroplane does not start on the appointed day but starts the next day, in that case also a telegram will be sent.

Article 24

This Agreement becomes valid as soon as it is signed.

Article 25

This Agreement will be valid up to Ist January, 1929.

Article 26

This Agreement has been drawn up in two texts, Russian and Persian, and both texts have equal force.

Dated 17th Hoot, 1306.

Muhammad Ihsan Khan,
Commandant, Afghan Air Force.

Jarinanoff,

Dated 7th March, 1928.

Head of the Dubrolet of the
U.S.S.R. Government.

VI—TREATY OF NEUTRALITY AND NON-AGGRESSION BETWEEN AFGHANISTAN AND SOVIET RUSSIA

(Kabul: June 24, 1931)

Translation

The Central Executive Committee of the Union of Soviet Socialist Republics and His Majesty the King of Afghanistan, being desirous of strengthening the friendly and good neighbourly relations happily existing between the two countries on the basis of the Treaty signed at Moscow on February 28th, 1921, and being convined that these relations will continue to develop in future, thus contributing to the lofty aims of world peace, have decided to conclude the present Treaty, which is inspired by the same principles as the Treaty concluded at Pagman on August 31st, 1926, and have appointed for this purpose:

The Central Executive Committee of the Union of Soviet Socialist Republics.

Leonide Nicolaeitch Stark, Minister Plenipotentiary of the Union of Soviet Socialist Republics in Afghanistan.

His Majesty the King of Afghanistan.

His Excellency Faiz-Mohammed Khan, Minister for Foreign Affairs of Afghanistan.

Who, having exchanged their full powers, found in good and due form, have agreed on the following provisions:

Article 1

In case of war or of hostilities between either of the contracting parties and one or more third powers, the other contracting party undertakes to observe neutrality with regard to the former.

Article 2

Each of the High Contracting Parties undertakes to

abstain from any aggression against the other party or against territories in its possession, and not to undertake or to tolerate on the part of anybody whatsoever any act which might inflict political or military damage on the other Contracting Party. Similarly, each contracting party undertakes not to be a party to any alliances or agreements of a military or political character with one or more powers which might be directed against the other Contracting Party or in any financial or economic boycott or blockade directed against the other Contracting Party. Furthermore, in the event of a hostile attitude being adopted by one or more third parties towards either of the contracting parties, the other Contracting Party undertakes not only not to encourage such attitude but is under an obligation in its territory to oppose it together with any hostile acts and undertaking arising therefrom.

Article 3

The High Contracting Parties having recognized each other's sovereignty, undertake to abstain from any armed or unarmed intervention in the internal affairs of the other Contracting Party and shall categorically abstain from giving any assistance to and taking part in any intervention whatsoever on the part of one or more third powers which might take action againt the other Contracting Party. The Contracting Parties shall not tolerate and shall prevent in their territory the organization and activities of groups of persons and the activities of private persons that might be prejudicial to the other Contracting Party or prepare the overthrow of its form of Government or make an attempt integrity of its territory or proceed to the mobilization or recruitment of armed forces to be used against it. Similarly, neither party shall authorize or permit the passage and transport through their territories of armed forces, arms, ammunition, implements of war and any kind of war material directed against the other Contracting Party.

Article 4

In accordance with the above provisions of the present

Treaty, each of the High Contracting Parties declares that it has not had and has not at present any secret or public obligations in relation to one or more states which would be incompatible with the present Treaty and that during the entire period of validity of this Treaty, it will not enter into any treaties and agreements which are incompatible with the present Treaty.

Article 5

Similarly, each of the Contracting Parties declares that no obligations exist belween itself and other states in the immediate neighbourhood of the land or sea frontiers of the other party except such as arise out of instruments which have already been made public.

Article 6

Beyond the limits of the undertakings the conditions of which are laid down in the present Treaty, each of the Contracting Parties retain entire freedom of action as regards steps to be taken to establish all kinds of relations and alliances with third powers.

Article 7

The Contracting Parties recognizc that the settlement of all disputes or conflicts which may arise between them of whatever character or origin must always be sought solely by pacific means. With a view to amplifying the provisions of this Article, special agreements may be concluded between the Contracting Parties.

Article 8

The present Treaty is concluded for a period of five years and shall come into force at the moment of its ratification, which shall take place not later than two months after the date of signature. The exchange of the instruments of ratification shall take place at Kabul within one month after ratification of the Treaty.

On the expiry of the period of five years, the present treaty shall be automatically prolonged from year year, to each Contracting Party being entitled to denounce it at six month's notice. In case of denounciation of the Treaty as provided for in this Article, the Contracting Parties shall at the same time enter into negotiations regarding the renewal of the present Treaty.

Article 9

The present Treaty is drawn up in the Russian and Persian Languages. In respect of its interpretation, both texts are regarded as authentic.

Done at Kabul, the 24th day of June, 1931.

(Signed) Faiz-Mohammad Khan
(Signed) Leonide Stark

VII—POSTAL AGREEMENT BETWEEN THE KINGDOM OF AFGHANISTAN AND THE USSR CONCLUDED BY THE INDEPENDENT DIRECTORATE OF POSTS, TELEGRAPHS AND TELEPHONES OF THE AFGHAN GOVERNMENT AND THE NATIONAL COMMISSARIAT OF COMMUNICATIONS OF THE USSR WITH PROTOCOL

(Kabul: April 3, 1932)

An Agreement with regard to Postal communications between the Kingdom of Afghanistan with the USSR has been concluded by the independent Directorate of Posts, Telegraphs with Telephones of the Afghan Government and the National Commissariat of Communications of the USSR. In order to improve the communications between the Kingdom of Afghanistan with the USSR, the contracting parties have appointed the following persons to sign the present Agreement in accordance with Article V, Paragraph 2, of the Universal Postal Convention signed at London:

On behalf of the Independent Directorate of Posts, Telegraphs and Telephones of the Afghan Government:

1. Mr. Rahimullah Khan, Director of Posts, Telegraphs and Telephones.

On behalf of the National Commissariat of Communications of the USSR:

1. Mr. Seronokoff, Acting Director of Newspapers and Posts.
2. Madame Seryakoff, Director of the International Branch of the National Commissariat.

Article 1

Arrangements will be made for the organized and direct exchange between the kingdom of Afghanistan and the

Government of the USSR of ordinary and registered mail, that is letters, post cards, service communications (papiers d'affaires), printed matter and commercial samples.

Article 2

The Contracting Parties agree to allow to pass through their respective countries mails of all kinds in transit, that is those mentioned in Article 1 of this Agreement whether originating in the territories of the Contracting Parties or in that of any other country with which either Afghanistan or the USSR exchange mails. The transmission of mail in transit will be governed by the provisions of Chapter I, Article 1, of the detailed regulations attached to the Universal Postal Convention dealing with closed mails and correspondence a'decouvert.

Article 3

Mails will be exchanged at the following places on the Frontier:

Afghanistan — Kara Tapa and Pattakesar.

USSR — Kushk in Soviet territory and Termez.

Article 4

Transport of mails between the frontier posts mentioned in Article 3 of this Agreement will be carried out as follows :

From Pattakesar to Termez and from Kara Tapa to Kushk in Soviet territory by and at the cost of the Postal Department of the Afghan government, and from Termez to Pattakesar and Kushk in Soviet territory to Kara Tapa by and at the cost of the Postal Department of the Government of the USSR

Article 5

The exchange of mails and similarly the submission of

accounts between the contracting parties will be based on the provisions of the Universal Postal Convention and the Detailed Regulations for the execution of the Universal Postal Convention regarding the exchange of mails and the method of submission of accounts.

Article 6

For the purpose of accounts relating to mails (letters and post cards, service communications, printed matter and commercial samples) in transit through the territories of the contracting parties the following distance has been accepted:

(a) The distances across Afghanistan for the purposes of accounting for mails in transit will be considered to be less than two thousand kilometres.

(b) The distance across the USSR will be considered to be :

(i) In the case of mail for Persia, Turkey and western China less than three thousand kilometers.

(ii) In the case of mail for Poland, Latvia, Esthonia and Finland more than three thousand and less than six thousand kilometers.

(iii) In the case of mails for Mongolia more than six thousand as less than nine thousand kilometers.

(iv) In the case of mails for Eastern China, Japan and countries beyond, provided they are sent by way of Harbin, Kuan Chand (sic), more than six thousand and less than nine thousand kilometers. If they are sent via Vladivostock more than nine thousand kilometers.

Article 7

The Frontier Post Offices of both-Contracting Parties

are entitled to make enquiries and obtain information regarding lost letters, etc. and other matters connected with the exchange of mails in direct communication with the opposite Frontier Post Offices of the other Contracting Party.

Article 8

Service correspondence between the Central Administrations of the Contracting Parties will be conducted in the French language and that between Exchange Post Offices in the Persian and Russian languages.

Article 9

Bags used for the transport of mails must be strong and in good condition and will be returned to the sender by the first mail.

Article 10

Postal accounts between the Contracting Parties will be prepared in gold francs and settled every three months in American dollars at the current rate of exchange.

Article 11

Monies due to the either of Contracting Parties and converted into American dollars at the current rate of exchange of Gold Francs will, after examination of the necessary documents, be paid through the Deutsche Bank, Berlin, by the Independent Directorate of Posts, Telegraphs and Telephones of Afghanistan or the National Commissariat of communications of the USSR The cost of payment will be borne by the debtor party.

Article 12

This Agreement has been concluded for a period of three years should neither party denounce it within six months before the expiry of this period, it will remain in force for five years.

Article 13

This Agreement will come into legal force three months after signature.

Article 14

This Agreement has been drawn up both in Persian and Russian and both texts are equally authentic.

(Signed) Rahimullah,
B. S. Seronokoff,
E. F. Seryakoff.

Signed at Kabul the 14th Hamal 1311 (corresponding to the 3rd April, 1932).

PROTOCOL

The representatives of the Contracting Parties when signing the above mentioned Agreement concluded at Kabul on the 14th Hamal 1311 (corresponding to the 3rd April, 1932) agreed to the following Articles :

1. In view of the necessity for various reforms in the Postal Department of the Afghan Government and also improvements of those roads within the Kingdom of Afghanistan on which mails in transit will travel, the Contracting Parties agree that all the Articles of the above mentioned Agreement which deal with the exchange of transit mail shall remain in abeyance until the independent Directorate of Posts, Telegraphs and Telephones of the Afghan Government shall inform the Commissariat of Communications of the USSR and the office of

the Universal Postal Union at Barne of the completion of the reforms in the Postal Department and of the improvements to the roads mentioned above.

2. Direct exchange of mails between Frontier Post Offices as laid down in Article 3 of the Agreement will at present take place not less than twice a week.
3. Letters in transit will be despatched in accordance with Article III of the detailed regulations for the execution of the Universal Postal Convention.

(Signed) Rahimullah,
B. S. Seronokoff,
E. F. Seryakoff.

Signed at Kabul the 14th Hamal 1311 (corresponding to the 3rd April, 1932).

VIII—TELEGRAPH AND WIRELESS AGREEMENT BETWEEN THE KINGDOM OF AFGHANISTAN AND THE U.S.S.R. CONCLUDED BY THE INDEPENDENT DIRECTORATE OF POSTS, TELEGRAPHS AND TELEPHONES OF THE AFGHAN GOVERNMENT AND THE NATIONAL COMMISSARIAT OF COMMUNICATIONS OF THE U.S.S.R. WITH PROTOCOL

(Kabul; April 3, 1932)

With the object of improving and extending communications by telephone and wireless telegraphy between the government of the kingdom of Afghanistan and the Government of the U.S.S.R., the contracting parties have appointed the following persons to sign the present Agreement under Article XVII of the International Telegraph Convention.

On behalf of the Independent Directorate of Posts, Telegraphs and Telephones of the Afghan Government:

1. Mr. Rahimulla Khan, Director of Posts, Telegraphs and Telephones;

On behalf of the National Commissariat of Communications of the U.S.S.R:

1. Mr. Seronokoff, Acting Director of Newspapers and posts.
2. Madame Seryakoff, Director of the International Branch of the National Commissariat.

The representatives of both Parties having communicated their full powers and found them to be in due and proper order, have agreed to the following:

Article 1

The Contracting Parties agree to arrange for the exchange of telegraphic and wireless communications both transit and terminal between stations as under:

(a) Exchange of terminal and transit telegrams between Kara Tapa in Afghanistan and Kushk in Soviet territory;

(b) Exchange of terminal and transit wireless messages between Kabul, Mazar-i-Sharif in Afghanistan and Tashkent, Termez and Kushk in Soviet territory.

Article 2

The Contracting Parties agree that in the event of an increase in the number of telegraph and wireless stations within their respective territories the exchange of transit and terminal messages between these stations will be decided by mutual arrangement on the basis of this Agreement.

Article 3

The Contracting Parties agree that all matters not detailed in this Agreement should follow the instructions laid down in the International Telegraph Convention and the Service Regulations annexed thereto.

Article 4

The Contracting Parties agree that the use of cipher telegrams in accordance with Article XVI of the Service Regulations attached to the International Telegraph Convention whether despatched by telegram or wireless will be limited to their respective Governments. As regards telegrams in code the procedure mentioned in Article VIII of the Service Regulations attached to the International Telegraph Convention will be followed.

Article 5

The Contracting Parties agree that Service telegrams on post and Telegraphs matters between Telegraph Offices of the Contracting Parties and also meteorological telegrams will be sent and received free of charge.

Article 6

The Contracting Parties agree that half rates will be charged on Terminal Press Telegrams as defined in Article 67 of the Service Regulations attached to the International Telegraph Convention.

Article 7

The Contracting Parties agree to charge the following rates on terminal and transit telegrams and wireless messages:

(a) Afghanistan; per word of a terminal message twenty five gold centimes, and per word of a transit message, thirty five gold centimes.

(b) The USSR; per word of a terminal message, thirty-five gold centimes, and per word of a transit message, seventy gold centimes.

Article 8

Accounts between Telegraph Office of the Contracting Parties will be prepared in accordance with Article 12 of the International Telegraph Convention and Article 79 of the Service Regulations annexed thereto, in Gold Francs and will be settled every three months in American dollars at the current rate of exchange of Gold Francs.

Article 9

Monies due to either of the Contracting Parties and converted into American dollars at the current rate of exchange of Gold Francs will, after the necessary documents have been examined, be paid through the Deutsche Bank Berlin, by the Independent Directorate of posts, Telegraphs and Telephones of the Afghan Government or the National Commissariat of Communications of the USSR. The cost of payment will be borne by the debtor Party.

Article 10

Service communications between the Central Administrations of the Contracting Parties will be written in French language and those between exchange Telegraph Offices in the Persian and Russian languages.

Article 11

This Agreement has been concluded for a period of three years and if neither party denounces it six months before the expiry of this period it will remain in force for five years.

Article 12

This Agreement will come into legal force three months after signature.

Article 13

This Agreement has been drawn up both in Persian and Russian and both texts are equally authentic.

(Signed) Rahimullah
B.S. Seronokoff
E.F. Seryakoff

Signed at Kabul the 14th Hamal 1311, Corresponding to the 3rd April, 1932.

PROTOCOL

The representatives of the Contracting Parties when signing the above mentioned Agreement concluded at Kabul on the 4th Hamal 1311 (corresponding to the 3rd April, 1932) agreed to the following articles:

1. Until telegraph and wireless communication between various places in Afghanistan is completed and so

long as it as necessary to send via the USSR telegrams or wireless messages from one part of Afghanistan to another, the Government of the USSR will accept such telegrams and wireless messages and despatch them in transit through its territory to the office of destination in Afghanistan and will charge thirty-five gold centimes per word (that is, the terminal rate).

2. The Contracting Parties will pay through the Deutsche Bank, Berlin in accordance with Article 8 and 9 of the Telegraph Agreement, monies due on terminal and transit telegrams and wireless messages and also on the transit telegrams and wireless messages mentioned in clause I of this Protocol for which they are responsible after accounts have been prepared and balanced.

3. The provision of the former Agreement regarding free transmission of state telegrams and wireless messages of the Contracting Parties, will from the date on which the Telegraph and Wireless Agreement, dated the 14th Hamal 1311 (corresponding to the 3rd April, 1932), concluded between the Contracting Parties comes into force, become null and void.

4. The Articles of the International Telegraph Convention and the Service Regulations annexed thereto referred to in the Telegraph and Wireless Agreement are those which were revised at Brussels in 1928.

(Signed) Rahimullah
B.S. Seronokoff
E.F. Seryakoff

Signed at Kabul, the 14th Hamal 1311, Corresponding to the 3rd April, 1932.

IX—CONVENTION FOR THE DEFINITION OF AGGRESSION BETWEEN AFGHANISTAN, ESTONIA, LATUIA, POLAND, PERSIA, ROUMANIA, SOVIET RUSSIA AND TURKEY

(London, July 3, 1933)

His Majesty the King of Roumania, the President of the Estonian Republic, The President of the Latvian Republic, The President of the Polish Republic, The President of the Turkish Republic, The Central Executive Committee of the Union of Soviet Socialist Republics, His Imperial Majesty the Shah of Persia, and His Majesty the King of Afghanistan.

Being desirous of consolidating the peaceful relations existing between their countries, mindful of the fact that the Briand-Kellogg Pact, of which they are signatories, prohabits all aggression; deeming it necessary, in the interests of the general security, to define aggression as specifically as possible. In order to obviate any pretext whereby it might be justified; and nothing that all states have an equal right to independence, security, the defence of their territories, and the free developments of their institutions; and desirous, in the interest of the general peace, to ensure to all peoples the inviolability of the territory of their countries; and judging it expedient, in the interest of the general peace, to bring into force, as between the countries, precise rules defining aggression, until such time as those rules shall become universal; Have decided with the aforesaid objects, to conclude the present Convention; and have duly authorized for the purpose :

His Majesty the King of Roumania :
M. Nicholas Titulescu, Minister for Foreign Affairs;

The President of the Estonian Republics :
Dr. Oskar Kallas, Envoy Extraordinary and Minister Plenipotentiary in London;

The president of the Latvian Republics :
M. Waldemaras Salnais, Minister for Foreign Affairs;

The President of the Polish Republics :
M. Edouard Raczyaski, Permanent Delegate to the League of Nations, Envoy Extraordinary and Minister Plenipotentiary;

The President of the Turkish Republics :
Tevrik Rustu Bey, Minister for Foreign Affairs;

The Central Executive Committee of the Union of Soviet Socialist Republics :
M. Maxime Litvinoff, People's Commissary for Foreign Affairs;

His Imperial Majesty the Shah of Persia :
Fatollah Khan Noury Esfandiary, Charge d' Affaires in London;

His Majesty the King of Afghanistan :
Ali Mohammad Khan, Minister of Education;

Who have agreed on the following provisions.

Article 1

Each of the High Contracting Parties undertakes to accept in its relations with each of the other Parties, from the date of the entry into force of the present Convention, the definition of aggression as explained in the report dated May 24th, 1933, of the committee on security questions (politis report), to the Conference for the Reduction and limitation of Arnaments, which report was made in consequence of the proposal of the Soviet delegation.

Article II

Accordingly, the aggressor in an international conflict shall subject to the agreements in force between the parties to the dispute, be considered to be that state which is the first to commit any of the following actions :

1. Declaration of war upon another state;
2. Invasion by its armed forces, with or without a declaration of war, of the territory of another state;

3. Attack by its land, naval or air forces, with or without a declaration of war, on the territory, vessels or aircraft of another state;
4. Naval blockade of the coasts or ports of another state;
5. Provision of support to armed bands formed in its territory which have invaded the territory of another state, or refusal, notwithstanding the request of the invaded state, to take in its own territory, all the measures in its power to deprive those bands of all assistance or protection.

Article III

No political, military, economic or other considerations may serve as an excuse or justification for the aggression referred to in Article II (For example, see Annex).

Article IV

The present Convention shall be ratified by each of the High Contracting Parties in accordance with its laws. The instruments of ratification shall be deposited by each of the High Contracting Parties with the Government of the Union of Soviet Socialist Republics. As soon as the instruments of ratification have been deposited by two of the High Contracting Parties, the present Convention shall come into force between those two parties. The Convention shall come into force as regards each of the other High Contracting Parties when it deposits its instrument of ratification. Each deposit of instruments of ratification shall immediately be notified by the Government of the Union of Soviet Socialist Republics to all the signatories of the present Convention.

Article V

The present Convention has been signed in eight copies, of which each of the High Contracting Parties has received one.

In faith whereof the above-named plenipotentaries have signed the present Convention and have thereto affixed their seals.

Done in London, July 3rd, 1933

(L.S.) (signed)—N. Titulesu
(L.S.) (signed)—O. Kallas
(L.S.) (signed)—Waldemras Salnais
(L.S.) (signed)—E. Raczynski
(L.S.) (signed)—Tevfik Rustu
(L.S.) (signed)—Maxime Litvinoff
(L.S.) (signed)—Ali Mohammad Khan
(L.S.) (signed)—F. Noury Esfandiary.

Annex

To Article III of the Convention relating to the Definition of Aggression.

The High Contracting Parties signatories of the Convention relating to the Definition of Aggression, desiring, subject to the express reservation that the absolute validity of the rule laid done in Article III of that Convention shall be in no way restricted, to furnish certain indications for determining the aggressor; declare that no act of aggression within the meaning of Article II of the Convention can be justified on either of the following grounds, among others :

(A) The internal condition of a state :

e.g., its political economic or social structure; alleged defects in its administration, disturbances due to strikes, revolutions, counter-revolutions, or civil war.

(B) The international conduct of a state :

e.g., the violation or threatened violation of the material or moral rights or interests of a foreign state or its nationals; the rupture of diplomatic or economic relations; economic or financial boycotts; disputes relating to economic, financial or other obligations towards foreign states, frontier incidents not forming any of the cases of aggression specified in Article II.

The High Contracting Parties further agree to recognize that the present Convention can never legitimate any violations of international law that may be implied in the circumstances comprized in the above list.

(L.S.) (signed)—N. Titulesu
(L.S.) (signed)—O. Kallas
(L.S.) (signed)—Waldemaras Salnais
(L.S.) (signed)—E. Raczynaki
(L.S.) (signed)—Tevfik Rustu
(L.S.) (signed)—Maxime Litvinoff
(L.S.) (signed)—F. Noury Esfondiary
(L.S.) (signed)—Ali Mohammad Khan.

Protocol of Signature

It is hereby agreed between the High Contracting Parties that should one or more of the other states immediately adjacent to the Union of Soviet Socialist Republics accede in the future to the present Convention, the said accession shall confer on the state or states in question the same rights and shall impose on them the same obligations as those conferred and imposed on the ordinary signatories.

Done at London on July 3rd, 1933

(Signed)—Maxime Litvonoff
S. Salnais
N. Titulesco
Ali Mohammad Khan
F. Noury Esfondiary
O. Kallas
E. Raczynski
T. Ruetu.

Deposit of ratifications in Moscow :

Roumania	October 16, 1933
Poland	October 16, 1933
Soviet Russia	October 16, 1933
Afghanistan	October 20, 1933
Persia (Iran)	November 16, 1933
Latvia	December 4, 1933
Estonia	December 4, 1933
Turkey	March 23, 1934

Accession :

Finland	January 31, 1934.

X—SOVIET-AFGHAN AGREEMENT REGARDING THE CAMPAIGN LOCUSTS IN THE TERRITORIES OF THE CONTRACTING PARTIES

(Kabul; May 6, 1935)

Translation

The Government of the Union of Soviet Socialist Republics and the Government of His Majesty the King of Afghanistan, deeming it necessary to take the measures indispensable for the protection of crops against the damage caused by locusts, have appointed as their plenipotentiaries :

The Government of the Union of Soviet Socialist Republics : Monseur Leonidas Nicolatievitch Stark, Minister Plenipotentiary of the Union of Soviet Socialist Republics in Afghanistan;

The Government of His Majesty the King of Afghanistan Monsieur Faiz Mohammad Khan, Minister of Foreign Affairs of Afghanistan.

who, having communicated their full powers, found in good and due form, have agreed upon the following provisions :

Article 1

The two Contracting Parties shall prepare measure against locusts and put them into effect in their territories and more particularly in the districts bordering on the frontier between the two countries.

Article 2

The two Parties agree that "Measures against Locusts" shall be held to mean the following measures :

(a) Locating and registering in spring of deposits of locusts eggs;

(b) Destructive measures properly so called;

(c) Observation of the flight of Locusts and registration in summer of deposits of Locusts eggs;

(d) Training of a special staff for the campaign against Locusts, recruiting of workers, provision of means of transport and preparation and despatch of poisonous substances, equipment and other material to the sectors in which work is to be undertaken.

Article 3

The two Parties agree that each year they will take the measures provided for in Article 2 at the following times :

In the case of point (a), from February 15th to April, 15th;

In the case of point (b) immediately after the mass deposit of Locusts eggs (from April 5th-15th to May 5th-15th), the essential purpose to the work during that period being to take strong measures to prevent the locusts reaching a stage of development at which they are capable of flight;

In the case of point (c), from the time when the Locusts start flight (May 15th to 20th) upto September 1st;

In the case of point (d), during all the autumn and winter period, it being understood that the work in question must be finished by March 1st, at the latest.

Article 4

The destruction of Locusts shall be carried out by chemical methods and also in case of necessity by mechanical means.

Article 5

Each of the two Governments, immediately after the coming into force of the present Agreement, shall establish on its territory a permanent Board for the campaign against Locusts. This Board shall consist of three members.

In the Union of Soviet Socialist Republics the permanent seat of this Board shall be at the town of Termez.

In Afghanistan the permanent seat of this Board shall be at the town of Mazar-i-Sharif.

The respective Board of the two Parties shall meet every year in December at a place to be appointed by mutual Agreement between the two parties on the territory of one or other of the parties in an ordinary joint session.

(a) To take cognisance of communications concerning the execution and results of the measures taken during the past year against Locusts in their territories;

(b) To discuss the plan for the measures against Locusts to be taken during the forth-coming years, and to determine the quantity of poissonous substances and oil-cake which the Government of Afghanistan will require during that period for the destruction of Locusts;

(c) To discuss jointly and settle all questions connected with the campaign against Locusts.

Article 6

The joint sessions of the Boards shall be held alternately in the territory of each party.

If necessary, extra-ordinary joint meetings of the Boards may be held by Agreement between the two Parties; these meetings shall be held at places determined by joint agreement between the Parties on the territory of one or other of the parties.

Article 7

Withing[1] a period of ten days from the signature of the present Agreement, the first extra-ordinary joint session of the two Boards shall be convened in order to organize future work and discuss the plan of measures to be taken for the purpose of the Campaign against Locusts in 1935.

This first extra-ordinary joint session shall be held in the town of Termez in the territory of the Union of Soviet Socialist Republics.

Article 8

The Parties agree that in addition to the communications made under point (a) of Article 5 of the present Agreement they shall transmit to each other between April 1st and July 15th of each year information concerning the deposit of locusts' eggs in their territory, the progress of the campaign against Locusts and the possibilities of flight of Locusts. This information shall be communicated by telegraph twice a month to the Board of the other party.

Article 9

The Government of the Union of Soviet Socialist Republics hereby declares that it is prepared to supply to the Government of His Majesty the King of Afghanistan, at a reasonable price and on payment in cash, the necessary quantity of poisonous substances and oil-cake and apparatus and utensils for the destruction of Locusts to be used in carrying out the measures against Locusts on Afghan territory. The supply of these articles shall be effected in the manner decided upon during the joint session of the Board. At these joint sessions the Boards shall determine the quantity of poisonous substances and oil-cake necessary for Afghanistan and the time-limit within which, and the manner in which, they are to be delivered on the spot.

Article 10

In virtue of the present Agreement, the Government of His Majesty the King of Afghanistan shall, in case of need and in so far as it may consider it necessary, engage for its own account Soviet specialist in measures against Locusts with the status of foreign officials; the Government of the Union of Soviet Socialist Republics shall assist in the recruiting of such specialists among citizens of the Union.

The terms on which these specialists shall be engaged for work in Afghanistan at Afghan officials shrll be fixed at the first extra-ordinary joint meeting of the Boards of the two parties, as provided for in Article 7 of the present Agreement.

Article 11

The present Agreement is concluded for a term of three years. If one year before the expiry of the period of validity of the present, Agreement neither of the two Parties has notified its intention of terminating it or of modifying certain of its provisions, it shall each time be prolonged by tacit consent for a further period of three years.

Article 12

The present Agreement shall come into force on the date of signature.

The present Agreement is drawn up in Russia and Persian both texts being equally authentic.

In faith whereof the above-mentioned plenipotentiaries of the two Parties have signed the present Agreement and have thereto affixed their seals.

Done in duplicate at Kabul, the 6th day of May, 1935 :

(L.S.) (signed)—L. Stark
(L.S.) (signed)—Faiz-Mohammad Khan

XI—PROTOCOL, RENEWING THE TREARY OF RECIPROCAL NEUTRALITY AND NON-AGGRESSION BETWEEN AFGHANISTAN AND THE UNION OF SOVIET SOCIALIST REPUBLICS SIGNED AT KABUL ON JUNE 24, 1931.

(Moscow; March 29, 1936)

The Central Executive Committee cf the Union of Soviet Socialist Republics and His Majesty the King of Afghanistan, desirous of continuing to provide a firm basis for the development of the relations between their respective countries in the future, and of giving fresh proof of the unalterable nature and solidity of the friendly and neighbourly relations happily existing between them; nothing that the Treaty of Neutrality and Non-Aggression concluded between them on June 24th, 1931, at Kabul, has exercised a beneficial influence on the development of these relations; have decided to sign the present protocol and have for that purpose appointed their plenipotentiaries:

The Central Executive Committee of the Union of Soviet Socialist Republics;

M. Nikolas Nikolaievitch Krastinsky, Member of the Central Executive Committee, Assistant People's Commissary for Foreign Affairs;

His Majesty the King of Afghanistan;

His Excelency Faiz-Mohammad Khan;

Minister for Foreign Affairs of Afghanistan.

Who having communicated their full powers, found in good and due form, have agreed on the following provisions :

Article I

Notwithstanding anything to the contrary provided in regard to the period of validity and the conditions for the expiry of the Treaty of Neutrality and Non-aggression concluded at Kabul on June 24, 1931, between the Union of Soviet Socialist Republics and the Kingdom of Afghanistan, the said Treaty shall remain in force until March 29th, 1946 (9th Hamal 1325). After this date, the period of validity of the said Treaty shall be automatically prolonged year by year, each of the High Contracting Parties being entitled to denounce it, subject to six month's notice being given.

Article II

The present Protocol shall be ratified. It shall come into force on the date of the exchange of instruments of ratification, which shall take place at Kabul as soon as possible.

Article III

The present Protocol is drawn up in the Russian and Iranian languages both texts being authentic for its interpretation.

In faith whereof the above named plenipotentiaries have signed the present protocol and have thereto affixed their seals.

Done at Moscow, in duplicate, this 29th day of March, 1936 (9th Hamal, 1325).

(Signed) : N. Krestinsky
(Signed) : Faiz Mohammad Khan

XII—AGREEMENT BETWEEN AFGHANISTAN AND SOVIET RUSSIA REGARDING FRONTIERS, WITH PROTOCOL

(Moscow; June 13, 1946)

Translation

In order to strengthen the friendly relations happily subsisting between the two countries, and further to extend these in future, the Royal Afghan Government of the one part and the Union of Soviet Socialist Republics of the other part have decided to conclude the present agreement for which purpose there have been appointed as their plenipotentiaries:

(Here follow the names)

The above-named plenipotentiaries, after mutual presentation of their credentials, which were found to be in due and proper form, have agreed as follows:

Article 1

Where the rivers Oxus and Panj are navigable the frontier shall follow the thalweg of these rivers, and where the thalweg is not determinable shall follow the centre of the actual main channel (Persian "Farwarter"), where the River Panj is unnavigable the centre of the stream shall be considered to be the boundary line.

The Island of Aral, Paighambar, shall continue to form part of the territory of the Union of Soviet Socialist Republics, and the Island of Urtatagai shall remain a part of the territory of Afghanistan.

Article 2

From the village of Khamyab to the Zarfol riuulet the task of precise delimitation of the boundary line, in the light of the stipulations contained in Article 1 of this agreement, shall be assigned to a joint commission composed of three representatives from both the Contracting Parties. The Commission shall draw up a map of this boundry line, decided the ownership of the Islands and setup boundary pillars at places where they consider them necessary. The Commission shall further compile a detailed report on this boundary line and on the places where boundary pillars have been setup. The Commission shall commence its task within 3 months of this agreement coming into force. The protocols formulated by the Commission, together with its report and map of the frontier, shall be subject to ratification by the Government of both the Contracting Parties.

Article 3

Possession of the Island in the rivers Oxus and Panj, shall be determined by the Commission, referred to in article 2 of this Agreement as follows:

Where the river, Oxus and Panj are navigable the Islands situated between the thalweg or Centre of the actual main channel and the left bank of these rivers shall be allocated to Afghanistan; whereas such Islands as are, situated between the thalweg or Centre of the actual main channel and the right bank shall be allocated to the Union of Soviet Socialist Republics. Where the river Panj is unnavigable possession of the Islands shall be determined by the position of the boundary line.

Article 4

This Agreement shall be subject to ratification and shall come into force with effect from the day on which the ratifications are exchanged. The ratifications shall be exchanged at Kabul as soon after the agreement has been signed as possible.

Article 5

This Agreement has been drawn up in two copies, each

copy being in both the Persian and Russian languages. Both the texts shall be considered to have equal force.

Drawn up in Moscow on June 13, 1946, Corresponding to 23rd Jauza, 1325:

Sultan Ahmad
Representative of His Majesty
the King of Afghanistan.

Molotov
Representative of the Executive
Committee of the Union of Soviet
Socialist Republics Assembly.

PROTOCOL

Consequent on the signing of the Russo-Afghan Frontier Agreement of today's date, the Contracting Parties confirm that clauses 9 and 10 of the Agreement concluded between the Union of Soviet Socialist Republics and Afghanistan on February 28, 1921, are annulled and will, therefore, be considered as no longer in force.

This Protocol shall form a part of the Agreement of today's date.

Dated June 13, 1946 (23rd Jauza, 1325)

Sultan Ahmad
Representative of His Majesty
the King of Afghanistan

Molotov
Representative of the High Executive
Committee of the Union of Soviet,
Socialist Republics Assembly.

Chronology

February 20, 1919, Amir Habibullah assassinated in Laghman, Nasrullah proclaimed himself Amir in Jalalabad.

February 25, 1919, Amanullah, the late Amir's son, proclaimed Amir in Kabul.

February 28, 1919, Nasrullah arrested, Amanullah proclaimed sovereignty of Afghanistan.

April 7, 1919, Amanullah sends friendly messages to Soviet Russia and other countries.

May 7, 1919, Lenin received Barkatullah, an Indian Revolutionary, in Moscow as Afghanistan's first representative.

May 21, 1919, Amanullah's message delivered to Moscow.

May 27, 1919, Soviet Russia formally recognises the sovereignty of Afghanistan.

May 28, 1919, Afghan Delegation to represent the country in Paris Peace Conference under the charge of Muhammad Wali Khan crossed the Soviet-Afghan border.

June 4, 1919, Afghan Delegation arrived in Tashkent.

July , 1919, N.Z. Bravin, first Soviet official representative, arrived in Herat.

July , 1919, Lenin received some more Indian Revolutionaries in Moscow.

August 13, 1919, Leon Trotsky enquired about the military condition and material needs of Afghanistan.

August 14, 1919, Soviet Russia offered free military aid to Afghanistan.

September 4-12, 1919, N.Z. Bravin arrived in Kabul and was received by Amanullah, negotiations started between two countries for coexistence, mutual cooperation and good neighbourly relations.

September 20, 1919, Trotsky wrote to the Central Committee of the Communist Party of Soviet Union that Britain tries to unite Iran, Bukhara, Khiva and Afghanistan against Soviet Russia.

September 24, 1919, Afghan Delegation left Tashkent for Moscow.

October , 1919, Amanullah sent men and material to help the Amir of Dukhara.

October 10, 1919, Afghan Delegation arrived in Moscow.

October 12, 1919, Chicherin meets the Afghan Delegation.

October 14, 1919, Lenin meets the Afghan Delegation.

November 11, 1919, Y.Z. Suritz arrived in Herat.

November 27, 1919, Afghan Delegation left Moscow, Letter of Lenin to Amanullah for mutual cooperation and close ties.

December 19, 1919, Afghan Delegation arrived in Tashkent.

September 13, 1920, Preliminary Soviet-Afghan Treaty was signed.

September 24, 1920, Amir of Bukhara fled to Dushambe and developed contacts with anti-Soviet Basmachi bands in Eastern Bukhara.

February 28, 1921, Treaty of Friendship and mutual Cooperation signed by Afghanistan and Soviet Russia.

March 3, 1921, Letter from Chicherin to Mahmud Tarzi.

March 5, 1921, Amir of Bukhara seeks asylum in Afghanistan where he lived in Kabul till the end of Second World War.

April 20, 1921, Letter from Lenin to Amanullah.

June 3, 1921, Soviet-Russia promises to help in the modernisation and industrial developmet of Afghanistan.

July 6, 1921, Fedor Raskolnikov, Soviet Ambassador, arrives in Kabul.

August 14, 1921, Soviet-Afghan Treaty of February 28, 1921, ratified by Amanullah at Kabul.

1922, Amanullah was reported to have entered into secret correspondance with Enver Pasha.

June 17, 1922, *Ittihad-i-Mashriqi* announced new trends in the Afghan Foreign Policy.

June 29, 1922, Enver Pasha defeated by the Soviets in an encounter at Kafiran near Dushambe in Tadjikistan.

August 4, 1922, Enver Pasha killed in one of the skirmishes by a machine-gun bullet while leading a cavalry counter-charge against Soviet force.

, 1924, Soviet Russia despatched a commercial mission to Afghanistan which stayed there upto 1927.

October , 1924, Soviet Russia supplied five airplanes to Afghanistan.

October 23, 1925, Soviet Russia provided trade concessions to Afghanistan.

December 19, 1925, Soviet troops penetrated into the Utra Tagai Island to wash off the Basmachi bands, but Soviet action perplexed the Afghans.

1926, German Merchantile Firm established in Kabul.

1926, Soviet-Afghan negotiations for the conclusion of a trade agreement failed.

February 4, 1926, Utra Tagai issue liquidated by Soviet-Afghan negotiations.

February 28, 1926, Soviet troops evacuated the Utra Tagai Island and surrendered its possession to Afghanistan.

June 10, 1926, Amanullah assumed the title of King.

August 15, 1926, Soviet-Russia recognised the economic importance of Utra Tagai Island to Afghanistan, agreed to Afghan ownership of Island and signs a Protocol with this effect.

August 31, 1926, Treaty of Reciprocol Neutrality and Non-aggression signed by Afghanistan and Soviet Russia.

October , 1926, Soviet-Afghan negotiations for the supply of ammunition to Afghanistan.

November 28, 1927, Soviet-Afghan Agreement regarding Kabul-Tashkent Air Route.

December 10, 1927, to June 20, 1928, Amanullah visits various European and Asian countries including Soviet Russia.

March 7, 1928, Agreement between the Afghan Air Force and the Dubrolet of Soviet Russia.

May 2, 1928, Amanullah received at Soviet frontier by L.M. Karakhan.

May 3, 1928, Amanullah arrived in Moscow and Spent fifteen days in Soviet Russia.

October 2-6, 1928, Amanullah justifies his tour in a series of lectures delivered over a period of four days.

November , 1928, to October , 1929, Civil War in Afghanistan, Amanullah's efforts for the transformation of Afghan society opposed by reactionary, conservative and fundamentalist forces who were inspired by British imperialism, Soviet Russia was interested in the development of Afghanistan and wanted Amanullah to retain his throne.

November 7, 1928, News from Kabul confirmed rumours of insurrection in Afghanistan caused by opposition of King Amanullah's attempts to introduce modesnizing reforms.

January 14, 1929, Amanullah renounces throne in favour of his brother, Inayatullah, who abdicated only after three days.

January 18, 1929, A Kohistani (Tajik) highway man and bandit, Bacha-i-Saqao—son of a water-carrier, ascended the throne of Afghanistan as Habibullah II for a few chaotic months; in October, 1929, Bacha was overthrown and executed by Nadir Khan.

January 19, 1929, Amanullah proclaims himself King and hoists the Royal Standard at Kandahar.

April , 1929, Ghulam Nabi aided by Soviet Russia to fight for the cause of Amanullah.

April 20, 1929, Ghulam Nabi crosses River Oxus and captures Mazar-i-Sharif with his Turkmen and Uzbek supporters.

May 23, 1929, Amanullah leaves Afghanistan and fled to permanent exile in Italy, upon hearing Amanullah's flight Ghulam Nabi also retires across River Oxus.

May 30, 1929, Soviet Russia proclaims its non-inteference in the Afghan Civil War.

October 6, 1929, Bach-i-Saqao defeated.

October 9, 1929, Bach-i-Saqao fled from Kabul.

October 14, 1929, Kabul seized by Nadir Khan's troops.

October 16, 1929, Nadir Khan proclaimed King with the title of Nadir Shah.

October 20, 1929, Soviet Russia acknowledges the accession of Nadir Khan to the Afghan throne; Soviet Foreign Minister, Karakhan, replies to Afghan Foreign Ministery despatch dated October 19, 1929.

December , 1929, Litvinov declares the Soviet Policy of Non-interference in the internal matters of Afghanistan.

February 25, 1930, Kalinin replies to the Afghan Minister's statement on presenting credentials.

June , 1930, Soviet troops crossed River Oxus and penetrated into the Afghan territory as far as forty miles, not with any hostile design, but to look for outlawed Basmachi bandits.

November 21, 1930, Soviet apology to Afghan Council in Moscow for murder of the Afghan Consul in Tashkent.

April/July, 1931, Ibrahim Beg, notorious Basmachi bandit, driven across the Oxus into the Soviet territory, where he was captured by the Soviet troops and imprisoned.

June 24, 1931, Treaty of Neutrality and Non-Aggression signed by Afghanistan and Soviet Russia.

July 6, 1931, Nadir Khan shows his eagerness to conclude a commercial treaty with Soviet Russia.

July 8, 1931, Nadir Khan declares Afghanistan's policy of neutrality and friendship towards her neighbours.

August , 1931, Shah Mahmud, brother of the King, celebrated his victory against Ibrahim Beg, notorious Basmachi bandit commonly known as *Robinhood of Bukhara*, at the annual festival of Independence.

February , 1932, Afghanistan supported Soviet view point at Disarmament Conference.

April 3, 1932, Postal, Telegraph and Wireless Agreements signed between Soviet Russia and Afghanistan, which helped in the development of more close ties between two countries.

September 13, 1932, Exchange of Soviet-Afghan notes on frontier incidents.

December , 1932, About 80 supporters of Amanullah were reported to have arrived in Tirmiz along with Soviet assistance.

1933, Reports came about the arrival of Amanullah in Moscow, and of Ghulam Rasul in Merv with 50 supporters.

January , 1933, British reports about Soviet spying in Afghan Embassy at Moscow.

June 3, 1933, Treaty defining the Aggression signed between Afghanistan, Estonia, Latvia, Iran, Poland, Rumania, Turkey and Soviet Russia.

November 8, 1933, Nadir Khan assassinated by a student whose family was involved in political movements, Soviet attempt to keep Amanullah on the throne, Nadir's 19-year old son takes the throne as Zahir Shah and rules till 1973, Young King's uncles serve him as advisers until 1953.

Hashim Khan, brother of Nadir Khan, acts as Prime Minister of Zahir Shah. In reaction to the upheavals of the Amanullah period and Nadir Khan's assassination, initially believed to be part of a conspiracy, there was a harsh authoritarian clamp down under Prime Minister Hashim Khan, wha, childless, began grooming his nephew, Sardar (Prince) Mohammed Daoud, for eventual power.

November 14, 1933, Soviet Russia granted recognition to King Zahir Shah.

November 18, 1933, TASS statement on Soviet recognition to Zahir Shah's regime in Afghanistan.

, 1934, U.S. recognises Afghanistan.

March , 1934, Bank-i-Milli formed in Afghanistan which later sings Trade Agreements with Sovafgantorg—the Soviet Trade Commissar.

September 18, 1934, Soviet Russia joins League of Nations.

September 25, 1934, Afghanistan joins League of Nations.

September 27, 1934, Litvinov issues a statement on the entry of Afghanistan into League of Nations.

May 6, 1935, Soviet-Afghan Agreement concluded for joint control of locusts.

, 1936, Afghan Foreign Minister asked the British Government for information and papers regarding Russo-Afghan frontiers.

March , 1936, Afghan Foreign Minister Faiz Muhammad visits Soviet Russia.

March 29, 1936, Soviet-Afghan Protocol signed prolonging the Treaty of 1931 signed between the two countries.

June 11, 1936, Trade Agreement signed between Bank-i-Milli (Afghan National Bank) and Sovafgantorg (Soviet Trade Commissar).

September 27, 1936, Soviet State Banquent in honour of visiting Afghan War Minister, Shah Mahmud, and speech by K.E. Voroshilov.

, 1937, Lufthansa, German Airlines, started weekly service between Berlin and Kabul; it was the first regular air link between Afghanistan and Europe.

May 3, 1937, American Inland Exploration Company was given the concessions for the exploration and exploitation of oil resources in Afghanistan. With this started the U.S. penetration into that Kingdom of Hindukush.

July 7, 1937, Saadabad Pact signed by Afghanistan, Iran, Iraq and Turkey.

July 10, 1937, Soviet Russia hailed the Saadabad Pact.

April 25, 1938, Soviet Russia and Afghanistan agreed to close down their respective consulates in Mazar-i-Sharif and Tashkent because of sensitive political situation in the region.

May , 1938, Afghan Air Officials send to Soviet Russia and other countries for advanee courses.

June , 1938, Shami Pir fails in attempt to regain the Afghan throne for Amanullah.

, 1936-1945, World War II, Afghanistan remains neutral but friendly to Allies despite inducements from the Axis Powers to aid an attack on British India. However, the refugees from Nazi Germay were given sanctuary.

, 1939, Oxus river boundary question raised by Soviet Russia with Afghanistan.

September 7, 1939, Afghanistan declares neutrality in World War II.

December 28, 1939, Reported activities of the Soviet and the Afghan troops in the border areas, but these reports were found nothing more than German propaganda to disturb the Soviet-Afghan relations.

, 1940, Hitler and Stalin together toyed briefly with the idea of restoring Amanullah to the Afghan throne.

July 29, 1940, Trade Agreement signed between Bank-i-Milli (Afghan National Bank) and Sovafgantorg (Soviet Trade Commissar).

August 17, 1940, In his statement to National Assembly, Zahir Shah declares neutrality of Afghanistan in World War II.

July 28, 1941, Afghanistan reaffirms its neutrality in World War II.

October 11, 1941, Soviet Minister in Kabul complains against the anti-Soviet activities of Axis nationals in Afghanistan.

October 17, 1941, Soviet Russia demanded for the expulsion of Axis nationals within one month from Afghanistan.

October 19, 1941, Afghanistan agrees to expel the Germans and the Italians from its territory on the Soviet and British demand.

, 1942, First U.S. representation in Kabul.

May 26, 1942, Treaty of Alliance signed between Soviet Russia and Great Britain.

November 5, 1942, Afghanistan reaffirms neutrality in World War II.

June 13, 1946, Frontier Agreement signed between Afghantstan and Soviet Russia.

November 5, 1946, United Nations General Assembly approves entry of Afghanistan.

November 19, 1946, Abdul Hussain Aziz takes seat as Afghanistan's first representative in United Nations.

, 1947, Britain withdraws from India after dividing it on religious grounds, As a British legacy, Pakistan continues to support fundamentalist and conservative elements in

Afghanistan, and inspire the terrorist activities to dominate the political scene in that country. For creating the trouble in Afghanistan and other parts of this region, Pakistan in supported and inspired by imperialist forces. In fact the birth of Pakistan was meant to inspire and develop terrorist activities in this region.

Bibliography

I. National Archives of India, New Delhi

(A) Foreign and Political Department Proceedings 1918-1939.

(i) External	B
(ii) Frontier	B
(iii) Mid-Asia	B
(iv) Near East	B
(v) Secret	E
(vi) Secret	F
(vii) War	B

(B) External Department Proceedings 1940-1945.

(i) Frontier	B
(ii) Near East	B
(iii) War	B

II. Articles

Bird, Alice, "Afghanistan as an Independent Power," "Interview with Muhammad Wali Khan," *The Modern Review*, July, 1921.

Castagne, Joseph, "Soviet Imperialism in Afghanistan", *Foreign Affairs*, July, 1935.

Chokaiev, Mustapha, "The Bolsheviks and Afghanistan", *Asiatic Review*, July, 1929.

Chokaiev, Mustapha, "The Situation in Afghanistan", *Asiatic Review*, April, 1930.

Conolly, Violent, "Soviet Union and the Industrialization of Asia", *Foreign Affairs*, October, 1936.

Davidson-Houston, J.V., "Russia in Asia", *Journal of Royal Central Asian Society*, Vol. 33, 1946.

Fletcher, Arnold, "Afghanistan: Highway of Conquest", *Current History*, January, 1950.

Fraser-Tytler, Sir W.K., "Afghanistan: A Brief Description", *Journal of Royal Central Asian Society*, Vol. 29, 1942.

Fraser-Tytler, Sir W.K., "The Expulsion of Axis Nationals from Afghanistan", *Survey of International Affairs, 1939-1946*, 1952.

Ghosh, N.N., "The Afghan Civil War 1928-29", *The Modern Review*, February, 1930.

Khan, Abdul Qadir, "Afghanistan since the Revolution", *Journal of Central Asian Society*, Vol. 17, 1930.

Khan, Abdul Qadir, "The Outlook in Afghanistan", *Journal of Royal Central Asian Society*, Vol. 19, 1932.

Khan, Abdul Qadir, "Afghanistan in 1934", *Journal of Royal Central Asian Society*, Vol. 22, 1935.

Maillart, E., "Afghanistan's Rebirth", Interview with Hashim Khan in 1937, *Journal of Royal Central Asian Society*, April, 1940.

Metta, Vasudeo B., "Changing Afghanistan", *United Empire*, November, 1939.

Mitrokhin, L., "Lenin and the Revolutionaries of the East", Interview with Raja Mahendra Pratap in 1979, *Soviet Review*, Vol. 17, No. 19, April 21, 1980.

Roome, Clive J., "The Future of Afghanistan", *The Near East*, March 7, 1919.

Shah, Ikbal Ali, "Afghanistan in 1919", *Journal of Central Asian Society*, Vol. 7, 1920, Reprinted in Germany, 1963.

Shridharani, Krishnalal, "The Frontier Gandhi", *Asia*, September, 1941.

Sykes, Sir Percy, "Afghanistan: The Present Position", *Jourual of Royal Central Asian Society*, Vol. 27, 1940.

Wilber, Donald N., "Afghanistan: Independent and Encircled", *Foreign Affairs*, April, 1953.

III. Journals

Asia (New York)
Current History (Philadailiphia)
Foreign Affairs (New York)
Journal of the Central Asian Society (London)
Journal of the Royal Central Asian Society (London)
Soviet Review (New Delhi)
Socialism (Moscow)
Survey of International Affairs (London)
The Asiatic Review (London)
The Modern Review (Berlin)
The Near East (London)
United Empire (London)

IV. Newspapers

Aman-i-Afghan (Kabul)
Daily Telegraph (London)
Frankfurther Zeitung (Germany)
Islam (Kabul)
Izvestia (Moscow)
New York Times (New York)

Pioneer (Allahabad)
Pravda (Moscow)
The Times (London)
Zaria Vostoka (Tiflis)

V. Books

Adamec, L.W., *Afghanistan's Foreign Affairs to the mid-twienth Century*, Relations with the USSR, Germany and Britain; Arizona (USA), 1974.

Adamec, L.W., *Afghanistan 1900-1923*, A Diplomatic History; Los Angeles, 1967.

Adhikari, G. ed., *Documents of the History of the Communist Party of India*, New Delhi, 1971, (Vol. I, 1917-1922).

Agabekow, George, *O.G.P.U. The Russian Secret Terror*, New York, 1931.

Aitchison, C.U. (Comp.), *A Collection of Treaties, Engagements and Sanads Relating to India and Neighbouring Countries*, 14 Vols., Calcutta, 1933, (Vol. 13, 1929-1933).

Ali, Mohammad, *Progressive Afghanistan*, Lahore, 1933.

Ali, Mohammad, *Afghanistan: The War of Independence*, 1919, Kabul, 1960.

Balfour, Lady Betty, *The History of Lord Lytton's Indian Administration 1876-1880*, London, 1899.

Batsell, W.R., *Soviet Rule in Russia*, New York, 1929.

Beloff, Max., *The Foreign Policy of Soviet Russia 1929-1941*, 2 Volumes, London, 1955. (Vol. I).

Carr, E.H., *International Relations Between the Two World Wars 1919-1939*, London, 1955.

Carr, E.H., *Fundamental of Planned Economy 1926-1929*, A History of Soviet Russia, Vol. III, London, 1978.

Dallin, David J., *Soviet Russia's Foreign Policy 1939-1942*, New Haven, 1942.

Dallin, David J., *The Rise of Russia in Asia*, London, 1950.

Degras, Jane, ed., *Soviet Documents in Foreign Policy*, 2 Vol. London, 1951-52.

Dupree, Louis, *Afghanistan*, New Jersey, 1973.

Elliot, J.G., *The Frontier 1839-1947*, London, 1968.

Eudin, X.J. and North, R.C. eds., *Soviet Russia and the East 1920-27*, A Documentary Survey, California, 1964.

Fedoseyev, P.N. ed., *Afghanistan: Past and Present*, Moscow, 1981.

Fischer, Louis, *Soviets in World Affairs*, 2 Volumes, London, 1930.

Fischer, Louis, *The Life of Lenin*, New York, 1964.

Fox, Ernst F., *Travels in Afghanistan*, New York, 1943.

Fraser-Tytler, Sir W.K., *Afghanistan: A Study of Political Developments in Central Asia*, London, 1950.

Ganjoo, Satish, *Afghanistan's Struggle for Resurgence*, Delhi, 1989.

Grassmuch, George, ed., *Afghanistan, Some New Approaches*, Michigam (Ann Arbor), 1969.

Gray, G.D.B., *Soviet Land*, London, 1947.

Great Britain, *British and Foreign State Papers 1812-1960*, 164 Volumes, London, 1841-1967. (Vols. 114/1921 and 146/1946).

Gregorian, Vartan, *The Emergency of Modern Afghanistan*, California, 1969.

Gromyko, A. ed., *History of Soviet Foreign Policy 1917-45*, Moscow, 1969.

Guha, Amalendu, ed., *Central Asia*, Delhi, 1970.

Hirszowics, Lukaz, *The Third Reich and the Arab East*, London, 1966.

Hamilton, Angus, *Afghanistan*, London, 1906, Boston, 1910.

James, Ben, *Afghan Journey*, London, 1935.

Kaushik, Devendra, *Central Asia in Modern Times*, Moscow, 1970.

Kennedy, Malcolm D., *A Short History of Communism in Asia*, London, 1957.

League of Nations, *Treaty Series*, Publications of the Treaties and International Engagements, Registered with the Secretariat of the League, Sept., 1920, July 31, 1946, 205 Volumes, London, 1920-1946.

(Vols. 14/1922-23. 21/1923-24, 62/1927, 105/1930, 147/1934, 154/1934-35, 157/1935, 164/1935-36, 177/1937, 190/1948).

Lenin, V.I., *The National Liberation Movement in the East*, Moscow, 1957.

Lewis, Bernard, *Turkey Today*, London, 1940.

Meijer, Jan M. ed., *The Trotsky Papers 1917-1922*, London, 1964.

Mitrokhin, Leonid, *Lenin and Indian Freedom Fighters*, New Delhi, 1988.

Ovsyany, I.D. ed., *A Study of Soviet Foreign Policy*, Moscow, 1975.

Rahul, Ram, *Politics in Central Asia*, Delhi, 1973.

Reyser, I.M., *Afghanistan*, Moscow, 1929.

Royal Government of Afghanistan, *The Five Years Economic Development Plans of Afghanistan*, Mimezaped, Kabul, 1956.

Russell, Ken (Tr.), *History of the USSR*, 3 Vols, Moscow, 1977, (Vol. III).

Sareen, Anuradha, *India and Afghanistan*, Delhi, 1981.

Shah, Ikbal Ali, *Tragedy of Amanullah*, London, 1933.

Shah, Ikbal Ali, *Modern Afghanistan*, London, 1939.

Smirnov, I.I. ed., *A Short History of the USSR*, 2 Parts, Moscow, 1965, (Part I).

Sontag, R.J. and Beddie, J.S. eds., *Nazi-Soviet Relations 1939-1941*, Washington, 1948.

Spector, Ivar, *The Soviet Union and the Muslim World 1917-1956*, Mimeographed, USA, 1956.

Stewart, R.T., *Fire in Afghanistan, 1914-1929*, New York, 1973.

Sykes, Sir Percy, *A History of Afghanistan*, 2 Vols, London, 1940.

Tate, G.P., *The Kingdom of Afghanistan*, Published in 1911, Reprinted, Delhi, 1973.

Triska, Jan F. and Slusser Robert M., *The Theory, Law and Policy of Soviet Treaties*, California, 1962.

USSR Tody and Tomorrow, Moscow, 1959.

Vaidik, Ved Pratap, *Afghanistan Men Soviyat-Ameriki Prati-spardha*, Hindi Delhi, 1975.

Vaidyanath, R., *The Formation of the Soviet Central Asian Republics*, New Delhi, 1967.

Violed, Ronald, *Amanullah Ex-King of Afghanistan*, London, 1932.

Volkov, Y. (Comp.), *The Truth About Afghanistan*, Moscow, 1980.

Wesson, Robert G., *Soviet Foreign Policy in Perspective*, USA, 1969.

Wilber, Donald N. ed., *Afghanistan*, New Haven, 1956, Second Edition in 1962.

VI. References

Statesman's Year Books, 1901, 1902, 1903, 1904, 1905, 1906, 1907, 1912, 1915, 1919, 1921, 1923, 1925, 1944.

Whitakar's Almanack, 1930.

Kaboul Alamanack, 1939-1940, 1941-1942.

Index